Besieged by the Boers

THE EFFECT OF A 100LB. SHELL

Besieged by the Boers

The Diary of a Doctor Within Kimberley
During the Second Boer War, 1899

Evelyn Oliver Ashe

LEONAUR

Besieged by the Boers
The Diary of a Doctor Within Kimberley
During the Second Boer War, 1899
by Evelyn Oliver Ashe

First published under the title
Besieged by the Boers

Leonaur is an imprint
of Oakpast Ltd

ISBN: 978-0-85706-276-5 (hardcover)
ISBN: 978-0-85706-275-8 (softcover)

http://www.leonaur.com

Publisher's Notes

The opinions of the authors represent a view of events in which he
was a participant related from his own perspective,
as such the text is relevant as an historical document.

The views expressed in this book are not necessarily
those of the publisher.

Contents

To My Mother
At Home in England
I Wrote This Diary,
Day by Day,
With No Idea of Ever Publishing it.
Now That I am Led to Change My Plan,
to Her I Dedicate This Book.

Kimberley,
March 6, 1900.

My hearty thanks are due to Mr. Marcus Bennett, Mr. C. Evans, Mr. F. H. Hancox and Dr. Stoney for the beautiful and interesting photographs with which they have kindly permitted me to illustrate this diary.

E.O.A.

Introduction

Kimberley is the second largest town in Cape Colony, and is the largest diamond mining centre in the world. It came into existence in 1870 with the discovery of diamonds, and, including its suburbs of Kenilworth, Beaconsfield, and Wesselton, has now a population of about 40,000, of which 25,000 are white. The three principal mines— Kimberley, De Beers, and Wesselton—are worked by the De Beers Consolidated Mines, Limited. This immense Company, of which Mr. Rhodes is the Chairman, has a capital of nearly four millions; pays well over a million a year in wages, and turns out ten thousand pounds' worth of rough diamonds every working day. All Kimberley makes its living directly or indirectly from the Company, and for all practical purposes Kimberley and the Company are one.

The town is 647 miles by rail from Cape Town and 485 from Port Elizabeth, and there is no English town nearer than the last named place. The Cape Town to Buluwayo Line passes through the town, but from the Orange River (seventy miles south of Kimberley) it runs for quite 400 miles close to the Orange Free State and Transvaal borders, never more than ten miles, often only two or three away from them. Kimberley itself is about four miles from the border. From its isolated position it could therefore be cut off with the greatest ease, and only relieved with the greatest difficulty, while the chance of looting its shops and well-furnished private houses naturally have had an irresistible attraction for the pious Boer and his still more pious *vrouw*.

CHAPTER 1

The Boers Strike First

Kimberley, November 19, 1899.

Goodness only knows when this will get posted, for it is five weeks today since we were cut off from the outside world, and though all along we have been hearing of troops on the way to relieve us, they are just as far off as ever, for all we know. I think, therefore, that as there will be such heaps to write about when we are relieved, I had better be getting some of it jotted down.

My last letter was written on October 8th, the day after we had had the parade of all our defence forces. Things went along quietly the first part of the next week, though we kept hearing plenty of rumours as to the Boer movements; but on Thursday, October 12th, the war really began, near Mafeking. Colonel Baden-Powell, who commanded there, seeing that war was inevitable, practically ordered all the women and children to leave, as he foresaw that Mafeking would have a very warm time of it.

They left in a special train, and an armour-plated train escorted it as far as Vryburg, and then started on the return journey. All went well till they got to Kraaipan, about twenty miles this side of Mafeking, and there the Boers had torn up the rails, so that the train ran off the road and came to a standstill. Then they pounded away at her with a small field-gun and rifles, until all resistance ceased, after which they took prisoners any men left alive and carried them off.

The first report we got was that the Boers had put a big gun slap in front of the returning train and blown the whole thing to bits, killing every soul in it; but this turned out not to be true, as the engine-driver managed to elude the Boers, and got away down to Vryburg and gave the correct version. Lieutenant Nesbit, who was in charge of the train, had been warned that the Boers held the line and that it was unsafe for him to return, but I suppose he thought there was just a chance of getting through, and so he risked it. He was reported to be badly wounded, but we have no further news of him so far.

This business considerably astonished us here in Kimberley, for though the people farther up country all said that war was certain to come, we did not at all believe it. The result, of course, was to increase the activity of the military, police, and Town Guard, and everything was done to hurry on our defences as quickly as possible. The 13th and 14th passed quietly without any alarm, but late on the night of the 14th (Saturday), a well-known man fetched me out to see his child, and told me news had just come in that the railway had been torn up at Spytfontein, about eight miles south of Kimberley. Next morning about 6.30 a.m., Stoney came in to tell me that the railway had also been cut at Riverton Road, ten miles north of Kimberley, and that the waterworks at Kiverton had been taken by the Boers and our water supply cut off, so we were practically in a state of siege. The alarm was to sound at about 9 a.m., and every one would have to go to his post. This was nice news, but all we could do was to make the best of it.

My first move was to fill up my big rainwater tank, the big bath, and every available receptacle, so that we should have a reserve to fall back upon in case of need; and most of the people did the same thing.

On the next day notice was given that, in order to economise water as much as possible (the reservoir in the town only holding enough for about three weeks), the supply would only be turned on from nine to eleven o'clock each morning, and that anyone found watering a garden or caught using water for anything except purely domestic and necessary purposes would have his supply permanently cut off, without respect of persons.

Quite early in the morning a big proclamation was issued, that from that time forward martial law was in force, and that no one would be allowed out of his house between 9 p.m. and 6 a.m. without a special permit.

All sorts of other subjects were touched upon in the proclamation, but that was the most important. I went round doing my work as usual, but at about 11 a.m. the "hooters" gave the alarm, and every one hurried off to his post. Many people had been warned and expected the alarm, but in the lower quarters of the town it came as a surprise, and there was quite a panic there. In some of the better streets, too, where a few excitable women lived near each other, there was a lively state of things, for they ran around frightening each other with yarns as to the number of Boers that could be seen advancing, and how very easily they could take Kimberley, and all the rest of it.

For some time before this the military people had been busy putting up earthworks and loop-holed forts all round the town—lots of them—in the most salient positions, such as on the tops of the *débris* heaps, and at the points which commanded the roads, etc. They had also formed a Town Guard—which nearly all the able-bodied men joined—of all ranks, and these men turned out to man the forts. We had only about six hundred Regulars here and about the same number of Volunteers and Volunteer Artillery, These had all been in camp for some days, but as the circle enclosed by the forts was *only* thirteen miles round, they could not anything like man the forts, so the idea was, and has been all along, that the Town Guard should man the forts whilst the Regulars, Volunteers, and Artillery were camped in a central position, ready to turn out sharp and proceed to any quarter upon which an attack was made.

Rumours kept flying around all the morning, but nothing happened. A patrol of the Mounted Police went out towards Riverton and was chased by a superior force of Dutch and had to leave behind two men whose horses were either shot or fell with them. One of the men I knew well, as he was the man from whom I always bought my horses. They were reported shot, but some days after we heard that they had only been made prisoners.

The armoured train went out both sides of Kimberley, and was fired on and had to retreat. And so it wore on to night, nothing happening but heaps of rumours and a good deal of scare all around.

Just before the outbreak Dr. Fuller decided to send his wife and family away to Cape Town, and he went part of the way with them. He had only just got back when he had a wire that his baby had been killed in an accident near Beaufort West, so off he went on Friday to his wife, passing Dr. Watkins on the way, the latter on his return from an English holiday. On the Saturday the railway was cut, and so Fuller could not return, but had to go on to Cape Town, and Watkins took his place to work with me at the hospital.

Rhodes turned up here, too, the last day the railway was open. Many people were wild with him, thinking that he would be an additional inducement to the Boers to attack us; but I think it was very plucky of him to come and stand by the town which made him, and with which he is so intimately connected. He did not stay idle long,

15

THE ARMOURED TRAIN

but began at once to raise a regiment of his own—the Kimberley Light Horse—paying for everything in connection with them out of his own pocket.

Next day (Monday, October 16th) was much quieter. Nothing had been seen or heard of the Dutch, and there were various rumours that relief from Orange River was close at hand, which quieted the people down a good deal.

The 17th was not a happy day for us altogether, though we heard that the Boers had been beaten back from Mafeking and lost many men. Nearer home we heard that the people at Vryburg and Warrenton were either too afraid or too disloyal to help the Mounted Police there, and as the latter were far too few to defend the places success-fully without the townspeople's aid, they retired on Kimberley, leaving Vryburg and the Fourteen Streams bridge at Warrenton over the Vaal River to the Dutch. The captain in charge of the Vryburg men was so broken down at having to retreat that it is reported he blew his brains out a few miles from Vryburg. The men at Fourteen Streams left their tents with lights burning in them, but brought everything else off safely. When morning came, the Dutch fired into the deserted camp for two hours, and then sent a *Kaffir* to see whether any one was left alive! They were surprised to find every one; had gone.

The two lots of police got in safely, *via* Barkley, on that day (Wednesday, October 1 8th). Nothing happened except that Agnes's troubles began. Heaps of people had rushed into town on the first day of alarm, and had no occupation or means of livelihood, and a relief committee was formed to inquire into their cases and help them if they were deserving. Agnes, always a too willing horse at any philan-thropic foolishness, commenced to work six hours a day at this game. After a few days she was dead beat, and so I cut the work down to three, and even that knocked her over after a couple of weeks. When there was a talk of relief, as usual lots of folks declined to work, but tried their best to get food for nothing.

One day over one hundred and sixty natives were told that if they wanted help they must work for it, and stone-breaking work was of-fered them. Three accepted it, and that was about the style of most of the people who applied for relief.

On Thursday, October 19th, there were all sorts of rumours about as to the railway having been broken all the way down to Hex River and that the Colonial Dutch had risen to join the Transvaal. This made a run on the provision stores, as if it were true, it meant that it would be a long time before we could get new supplies of food in. At least some people thought so, forgetting that most of our supplies come *via* Port Elizabeth, which is nearly two hundred miles nearer. Anyhow, there was a run on provisions, etc., and the storekeepers naturally put the prices up, and they did it with a vengeance. Paraffin, which had been selling at sixteen shillings and sixpence, went up to three pounds for a ten-gallon case, and other things in proportion. We had got in a fair stock of stuff previous to this, but I bought two sacks of flour to be on the safe side.

This tremendous run up of prices made it very hard on the poor, and so the military authorities took the matter in hand, and issued a proclamation next day that all prices were to be exactly the same as they were before the siege began. This was a very good thing, and of course they took good care to see that it was carried out by providing heavy penalties for anyone who did overcharge.

We have had plenty of military proclamations, but most of them have been quite wise, such as forbidding the sale of liquor to natives except during very limited hours, and later on absolutely prohibiting the sale of liquor to them at all. The bar-keepers did not like this last order, but after one of them was fined thirty pounds and got his bar completely closed till the end of the siege came, they saw that they had to obey it.

At about this time my new single-horse trap was completed, and I tried two of my horses in it and found they went very well. This was lucky, for horse-keep looked like getting dear, and as we were shut in, there was not so much work in the outlying places. I therefore thought that I would sell out all but my best horses, and do the work with three, or even two, if keep got to be too dear. I did the good citizen by lending one horse to the Volunteers, on condition that I was to have him back when things came right, but if he died or got shot, that was better than having him looted by some thieving Boer. I sold another horse to the Light Horse, and found that I could do my work with the three remaining ones quite well, running a single horse half the day and the old cart with a pair the other half.

About the first day I had the new cart out I had an amusing experience. After the first alarm the military people blocked up all the small streets leading into the town with barricades of old waggons, carts, water-tanks, and other heavy lumber, and where this was not available they put up strong, high, barbed-wire fences, eight or nine strands. This was, of course, to prevent any rushing of the town by the

KENILWORTH BARRICADE

Boers, and most of the barricades were artfully arranged so that if a rush were made the Boers would be blocked just under the forts or redoubts, from which our men could pot them with great comfort, both with rifles and Maxims, of which we had a good supply. Not that previous experience led us to believe that the Boers would be likely to rush us, as they prefer to be behind shelter and shoot at long range, and have far too great a respect for their own dirty hides to venture an assault. Another little surprise packet that was carefully arranged for them was to bury dynamite in the places that seemed likely for them to use as attacking points (of course at a safe distance from the forts), and arrange for the electrical firing of them when required.

This little dodge was diligently talked about and very soon got over to the Boers, but as no one but the initiated few knew just where the dynamite was buried, it left the Boers with the pleasant feeling that wherever they chose to attack it was just as likely as not that their worthless insides would be blown out by dynamite, which I have no doubt did not much increase their ardour.

The main streets were barricaded in just the same way as the small ones, but an opening was left in the centre, and a guard was put on either side of Volunteers or Town Guard or police (all fully armed), with orders to allow no one to pass in or out without a properly signed permit, and even then to search both their carts and pockets if they thought fit. The first day these orders were in force I wanted to see a patient about one hundred yards beyond one of the barriers. I did not know the orders, as no notice of them had been given, and when I got near the barrier I saw carts being stopped, so I said to the man on guard, "Are you going to stop me too?"

"Yes," he said, "unless you have a permit."

"May I leave my cart here and walk, over there to see the patient?"

"No; if you have no permit, neither you nor the cart can pass."

So I said, "All right, orders are orders; I will go and get a pass."

The joke was that the man on guard was a patient of my own and knew me well, but he was quite right.

On more than one occasion Rhodes has been stopped at the barrier, and asked for his permit; and at one barrier, where the orders were to search everybody, the guard stopped him and told him that he would have to be searched. Rhodes fumed and blustered, and said he had never heard of such insolence, but the guard was firm; so Rhodes burst out laughing and produced a permit to pass the barrier without

THE CONNING TOWER

being searched. He was just trying it on. Whatever else he may be, he is no coward; he goes through the barrier and rides far out on the *veldt* almost every afternoon with only one or two friends and no escort at all. He always wears white flannel trousers, and is most conspicuous. Nothing could save him if a Boer chose to lie in wait and pot him with a long-range shot; and as the Mauser rifle which the Boers use carries well over a mile, the shooter could be well in amongst his own people long before any of ours could get a chance at him.

That this could easily happen is shown by what did happen on October 20th. A patrol of the Mounted Volunteers (Diamond Fields Horse) was out scouting early in the morning; no Boers were seen anywhere about, when a shot was fired, and one of the sergeants fell off his horse—dead. The men hunted everywhere round about, but could not find a sign or footprint of anybody. The modern ammunition is smokeless powder, so no smoke was seen and no one knows who fired the shot.

On the same day we heard that the Boers had issued a proclamation declaring Bechuanaland to be Transvaal, and Griqualand West Orange Free State, territory; but of course our commander, Colonel Kekewich, promptly issued a counter-proclamation, warning all loyal subjects not to have any truck with such foolishness, as these territories were still British, in spite of the Boer proclamation.

Kekewich is the colonel in command of the Lancashires; he is a Devonshire man, though his name does not sound like it, and is a splendid fellow. Everybody likes him. He is the head of the whole business, and must have an anxious time, as he is responsible for everything. I think I told you that a big lookout had been put up on top of the most centrally situated mine-head gear. This must be about a hundred and twenty feet above the street level, and gives a splendid view of all the surrounding country; and here the colonel spends most of his day, watching what the Boers—and our own men too, for that matter—are up to. The top of this tower is in telephonic communication with all the forts, so that orders are sent from it to all points with great rapidity.

At night there are strong electric searchlights in commanding positions at the forts, and they are at work during all the dark hours, so that it is impossible for the Boers to make any advance without its being at once seen. That is the advantage of having an immensely wealthy company like De Beers' in the place, they have skilled mechanics and electricians, and machinery and appliances, to do almost anything, and a jolly mess we should have been in without them. As a matter of fact, though, we should never have been besieged but for the mines. The Boers openly gave out that they wanted to take Rhodes prisoner and to blow up his mines, and did not wish to injure anybody else.

After the first alarm the De Beers people brought in all or a great part of their cattle from their outlying farms, and herded about fifteen hundred of them just outside Kenilworth. Having failed to do much by cutting off our water supply, the Boers thought they would next try for our food supply, and I suppose their natural love of cattle stirred them up too, for if there is anything that a Boer will risk his immortal soul to get, it is cattle.

THE SEARCH AND SIGNAL TEAM – WESSELTON

CHAPTER 2

Fighting and Raiding

On Tuesday, October 24th, a patrol of our men was out, and ran across a strong force of Boers, whose object was evidently to raid these cattle. A brisk engagement ensued about six miles out. Reinforcements went out to our men, but owing to their being guided by a man who did not know the ground well, they got into difficulties, and were well peppered by a body of Boers who had taken up their position behind the bank of a dry dam, of the existence of which the guide was ignorant. The colonel, seeing there was likely to be a defeat, sent out some of the Lancashires in the armoured train, and they cleared the Boers out in style, and converted what was very nearly a disaster to our men into at any rate a drawn game. The Boers drew off, and so did we. The butcher's bill on our side was pretty heavy—three killed and about twenty-five wounded, four of them severely. Out of the wounded, three were officers, and two of them were severely damaged, the bullets having splintered up the thigh-bone in both cases.

The Boer loss was not, and never will be, known, but must have been pretty heavy. The only certain thing about it was that their commandant was killed. He was left on the field when the Boers retired, and, being a man from Boshof and well known in Kimberley, he was easily identified by our people. He was in Kimberley on the Saturday afternoon that all the forces were reviewed, and is reported to have rather sneered at the show, saying it would just be a nice handful for the Boers. Thank goodness he got his dose early, and as he was well known and popular among the Boers, his death jarred them up considerably.

We had a pretty busy time at the hospital when the wounded came in. I got five of them under my hands, but only two were more than trifles—an officer shot through the chest and a sergeant shot through the arm, splintering up the bone. We doctors had all of us seen a few bullet wounds with revolvers and such like, but had no experience of the modern rifle bullet, and it was a revelation to us. The bullet, especially of the Mauser rifle which the Dutch use, is so small and travels with such velocity that it drills clean through everything, and unless it strikes a vital part, or hits a bone or big artery, the injury it inflicts is ridiculous. The officer shot through the chest left the hospital on the eighth day, and returned to duty on the ninth, and his duty consisted of at least twelve miles' riding every day. Wounds through the fleshy parts heal in a couple of days, and give no trouble after a week.

But a Mauser bullet will drive clean through anything. One poor chap in another engagement was shot in the ribs of the right side, far back, and the bullet travelled right through him in a slanting direction and came out at the outer side of the left thigh, about its middle, cutting the spine right across on its way and completely paralysing him. He only lived a few hours. Another bullet in this Dronfield fight of which I have been speaking hit the ammunition box of the Maxim gun. The ammunition is carried in a stout canvas belt, like the leather thing they call a bandolier. The box is stout, and the cartridges are solid brass (not cardboard), and yet the bullet drove through the box, and through no less than ten cartridges, with the intervening twenty thicknesses of canvas, and none of the cartridges exploded.

After this brush, things were very quiet for several days. We got news of some of the Natal fights, and heard that the Boers had been repulsed from Mafeking every time they tried to take it, which encouraged us a good deal. There were many disquieting rumours, though, as to the strength of the Boers and the big siege-guns they were bringing to bombard us with. The alarmists talked glibly about forty-pounders, as if you could carry them about in your waistcoat pocket, though our artillerymen told us that a forty-pounder is so heavy that it would take about seventy mules or oxen to drag it. This, however, was a detail which the alarmists ignored. They could raise the mules right enough, but that they would get a heavy gun eighty miles across country without a foot of metalled road in the whole distance seemed to me too big a job for their size.

All on from October 8th we had beautiful rains at intervals of a few days, and the water came in very handy. I got in another big water-tank and arranged my water-pipes to run into it. During every rain I slopped around with a bucket and a mackintosh, filling every available receptacle just like old times at home. Our garden was coming on beautifully when we had to give up watering it, but the rains kept it just going, and I managed to keep the vines and vegetables alive with bath and slop-water. At first we filled the tanks and kept them as a reserve in case the water in the reservoir gave out before we were relieved, but by the time we had been shut up about three weeks the De Beers Company, as usual, came to the rescue.

One of their mines, Wesselton, has a big stream of underground water in it, and this water has for the last year or two been pumped into a dam at Kenilworth, from which it is taken to the floors and used for washing the "blue" or diamondiferous earth. In one place this water-main ran not very far from the water company's main, so De Beers' put on a lot of niggers and joined the two, and were then able to pump from Wesselton to the reservoir. So we had a good supply of water once more, much harder than our regular supply from the Vaal River, but quite good all the same, and quite sufficient for all purposes except watering gardens. After this supply was fixed up, we felt quite safe in using any rain-water we saved for the garden, and did so; but a good many of the shallow rooted things had died, though the vegetables were flourishing.

The first rumour about the waterworks had been that the Boers had blown up the pumping machinery on the first day of the siege, but this turned out to be incorrect. They took possession of it and of the enginemen, and were going to blow it up, but a wily engineman is reported to have said: "Why do you destroy your own property? When you have taken Kimberley, you will want a water supply just the same, and it will cost a good deal to replace the machinery." He went on to suggest that they could cut off the Kimberley water and do themselves a good turn at the same time by pulling up the pipes at a place six miles from the river where they ran through a pan which had water in it only after very heavy rains; then they could pump river-water into this pan, and thus have a watering place for their horses much nearer Kimberley. The Boers tumbled to this plan and carried it out. Of course the engineman's idea was to try and save the pumps if possible, but the Boers have laid dynamite ready to blow them up if they have to retreat, and they probably will do so unless the wily man manages to wet the dynamite.

The hotel-keeper at Riverton where we have stayed several times is said to be doing a roaring trade, as the Boers are paying him for all they take, but this was arranged by the commandant who was shot. He was a great friend of the hotel-keeper's. Whether this state of things will go on now, nobody knows, but the Boers are quite equal to demanding every penny he has and then shooting him when they retreat. That is what one is afraid of for the outlying people. So long as all goes well with them, the Boers may be fairly civil, but when they are beaten and have to retreat, there is no dastardly cruelty of which they might not be guilty. The cowardly brutes have said that in that case they intend to shoot men, women, and children. On the other hand, if they were to win, their programme, as laid down by their own rabble, is "to shoot all the Englishmen and to give their women to the *Kaffirs*." These are the people of whom Olive Schreiner writes, "The simple God-fearing farmer," etc., etc.

All this time we were, of course, under martial law and not allowed out between 9 p.m. and 6 a.m. without a permit. Many special constables were sworn in, and patrolled the streets at night in pairs, one with a rifle and the other with a revolver. At first they were very energetic, and it was "Halt! Who goes there? Advance one and give the counter-sign" at about every hundred yards. After a week or two they quieted down a bit, but are still fairly lively, particularly if you are in a cab driving at night. A few nights ago I was stopped in a cab by a most ferocious individual.

He yelled out: "Why don't you stop? If you don't stop the minute I challenge, be God I'll shoot!" At least, that was the sense of what he said, but his accent was beyond me; however, thinking it over, I came to the conclusion that he was either a Jew drunk on Scotch whiskey or an Irishman *ditto* with German beer.

After the Dronfield fight on October 24th nothing happened in the war department for a long time, but I was pretty busy medically, and a case of smallpox developed down in Beaconsfield, which made rather a scare, but the man and another man who shared his room were promptly taken out to the *lazaretto*, and no further cases developed.

On the 31st we received our first intimation that the Boers had got some artillery with them, as they fired some shots from a field-gun at a patrol of our men which was out in the Free State direction to the north-east of Kimberley, but no one was hit.

On November 1st about 2 p.m. we heard a tremendous explosion, and on looking round saw a huge column of smoke to the north, over the dynamite magazines, so we guessed that the Boers had blown up the De Beers' stock of dynamite, and this afterwards turned out to be true. This dynamite had been stored in the town, but the Town

Council got scared, fearing that if bombardment took place and a shell struck it, it would blow the whole town to bits, so they had it removed some distance out. The De Beers people used to fetch in what they wanted every day, but on this same morning the Boers had fired on them when they were going out, and so they had to return without any.

The Company was very angry with the Town Council about this, because they said that they could have kept the dynamite with perfect safety inside the town limits, by dividing it up into small lots, and keeping these in separate places. The mines had to be shut down very soon after this for want of dynamite, but it did not really make much difference, as they ran short of fuel only a few days after. On this same day, too, we started on brown bread by military order. There was a far larger stock of coarse meal than of flour in the town, so the colonel ordered the making of white bread to cease, and all the bread to be made of three-quarter meal and quarter flour.

On the 2nd a smaller dynamite magazine was blown up, but it only made a very small explosion compared with the first one. On this day a Jewish patient of mine amused me very much. He had a store out at Windsorton, but he and his family lived in Kimberley. He managed to get out to his store to see how things were going on, and the Boers had not interfered with him, beyond frightening the soul out of him with their boasting. They told him that they had shelled Mafeking and killed everybody in it, and that they were going to do the same for Kimberley. He came straight back to fetch his wife and family out to the store "for safety," though his wife had only been confined a fortnight. He must have been badly scared, for he said the Boers had commandeered a hundred pounds' worth of goods from his store, but "that is nothing." For a Hebrew to call a hundred pounds "nothing," means that he is off his head with funk. I asked him what the Dutch said of the Dronfield fight, and he replied that they had told him they had killed forty English, wounded one hundred, and captured one hundred and fifty horses.

"You know yourself," I said, "that four were killed and twenty-five wounded that day, so how can you believe them in other things when they lie so frightfully about the things you do know?"

To my great surprise, he decided to stay in town, but I did not at all expect he would be so sensible.

The next day (November 3rd) was a very anxious day. The alarm sounded at lo a.m., the Boers again trying to raid the Kenilworth cat-

29

tle, but after a good deal of long-range firing they were driven off, only one man of ours being wounded. The men had just got in, when another attack seemed likely on the opposite side of the town. There was pretty heavy fighting there for a couple of hours, and we got our first sound of artillery fire, our guns backing up our mounted men, and blazing away well. Between them they managed to drive the Boers off, with two men on our side wounded. Dr. Watkins got a man wounded through the right lung, who ultimately did quite well, and I got a poor chap who was shot in the side of the head, and who died on the operating-table as I was seeing if anything could be done for him.

The sanitary system here is a pail system. All the closets have pails, and these are taken away, and fresh ones put in, every other night. The full pails are carted away in big covered vans that always remind me of the menagerie vans that used to come through Garton on the way from Roos to Aldborough. There are a good many of these vans, and they take a lot of oxen to draw them. The work is done by short-sentence native prisoners, under proper guards, and vans, oxen, and natives—in fact, the whole plant—are kept at a big compound, a mile from town.

On this afternoon the Boers made their attack from this quarter, and began by raiding all the vans and the oxen that pulled them. This looked like altogether disorganising the sanitary service, and in the afternoon edition of the paper (a piece the size of a single sheet of notepaper, price three pence) a request was issued to all householders to dig holes three feet deep in their gardens or yards, and empty their pails into them, adding a covering of earth. This looked all right, but how to dig a three-foot hole when eighteen inches brought you down to solid rock, as it does in some parts of the town, was not explained by the authorities. Then, again, for every man who would carry this scheme out properly, there would certainly be ten who were too idle or careless to bother about it. On the face of it, this plan was no good. I did my own scavenging for one day, but then the sanitary contractors managed to carry out their work with other plant, and so this difficulty was got over.

On the next day everything started quiet, but the De Beers' steam "hooter" went at noon, because a party of Boers were hovering round Wesselton in a threatening way. Our people dropped a few shells about their ears, and they concluded that they did not want Wesselton as badly as they had thought. On this day (November 4th) we heard

LIEUTENANT-COLONEL R. G. KEKEWICH

of the twelve hundred men in Natal who had pursued the Boers too far and been obliged to surrender when their ammunition gave out, and very sick we felt about it. I also heard of the packet of dynamite that had been found under the big bridge in the centre of the town. A policeman went under the bridge, and some men scuttled away, leaving a parcel behind them which turned out to be dynamite. As a matter of fact, unless a hole had been drilled deep and the dynamite properly put in it, there was not enough to burst the bridge. But it showed plainly what we all knew quite well, that we had traitors in the camp.

When the trouble first began, and martial law was proclaimed, a court-martial was established. Its members were partly Army officers, and partly civilians. The civilians were the resident magistrates of Kimberley and Beaconsfield, the Civil Commissioner of Kimberley, and one of the High Court judges. This court tried all people who broke the martial law provisions, such as those who were out after hours without permits, who broke through the barriers, or had arms in their possession illegally, or who were in any way in communication with the Boers. In theory the constitution of the court seemed all right, but in practice it was absurd. The military members were too full of more important work to attend, and so the civilians had it all their own way. They were all men who had to do with civil law cases, and consequently were always wanting minute and conclusive evidence before they convicted a man. That is all right in civil work, but it is no use in a case like ours. What was wanted was a court of men who knew no law, but understood common sense. A court like this would have decided that if there was the shadow of suspicion against a man, it would be safer to gaol him out of harm's way until the siege was over.

But this court was ruled by the superior officer of the others in ordinary times, and most offenders were dismissed with a caution. Everybody was very disgusted with the court in consequence. On one occasion some men were seen on a *débris* heap waving flags to the Boers, whilst they (the Boers) were actually firing shells into the town. Some police went and collared the men, and then this extraordinary court asked the police whether they could positively swear that their captures were the men who waved the flags. As the heap was half a mile off, of course the police could not swear to them, so they were dismissed with the usual caution.

On this same day (November 4th) there was a rumour that the Boers had sent an "ultimatum" to the colonel that if he did not surrender in twenty-four hours, they would bombard the town. Whether true or not, this yarn was widely believed, and many people expected the shelling would begin at daybreak on the 6th, but it did not. They fired two shells at sunset at Wesselton mine, and we thought we were in for a night bombardment. The hooters went, and every one turned out to his post, but nothing happened.

This was the last we heard of the hooters, and everybody was glad. It was a weird, ghastly sounding alarm, and scared nervous people out of their senses, so the colonel stopped it and instituted a cone alarm, like a wind cone on a pier, but so far I have never seen it. The hooter was the one used to tell the miners their time, and we were used to two blasts from it when the shifts changed, three times a day, but the three blasts frequently repeated during this part of the siege fairly gave one the horrors, especially at night. It will be a long time before we forget those three blasts, and when things are settled and we start our usual two again, it will be some time before we give up pricking up our ears and listening for the third hoot when we hear the first two.

CHAPTER 3

The Bombardment Begins

Our long-expected bombardment began on the next day (November 7th), and it was a feeble business. The Boers fixed a gun on a *kopje* about four miles out Spytfontein way, and commenced trying to shell us. They fired about twenty shells in all, and no damage whatever was done. A very few—only two or three—reached the town, and they fell in the street, and no injury whatever was done either to people or property. The gun was so far off that we could not hear much of a report when it went off, and the shells burst with an insignificant noise—that is, when they did burst at all, but the majority of them did not burst. The corruption of the Boer Government had recoiled on themselves, and whoever supplied the shells had supplied apparently a job lot of old stuff, and had no doubt charged full price, and a little over, for them.

Report says that some of the shells which did not burst were filled with sawdust instead of powder, but I do not know whether this is really true or not. One shell fell in the same street as Ruffel's shop, where my office is, but about one hundred and fifty yards higher up. It is said to have exploded within a few yards of an Irish policeman, but all the notice he took of it was to remark, "Begob, fwhat will they be playin' at next?" For the truth of this, however, I will not be responsible either. Several of these shells fell not far from the house of a patient of mine, which is in a prominent position and easy to see from a distance; but the lady of the house sat quietly on the verandah without turning a hair, being rather amused than otherwise. She gave me a chunk of one of the shells as a memento.

Next day we were waked before six by three cannon shots which sounded very close, and after the shot we could hear the shell explode each time, so we thought that the Boers had got hold of a better lot of

34

stuff, and really meant business this time, but it turned out afterwards that it was our own guns firing.

On the 9th Agnes started with influenza, and had to give up her refugee work at last. I was very busy, and could not look after her much myself, so I got a nurse to attend to her, and she got all right in a few days.

The 10th was a quiet day. No bombarding took place, but the armoured train was fired on by the Boers as it went to try and reconnoitre to the northward.

Next day (the 11th) we had a pretty hot time. The Boers had brought their guns nearer and to a different position, and began shelling at 5.15 a.m. They had got the range by this time, and almost every shell landed in the town. I had to go out early to a case, and went down into the main road opposite the end of the house, and stood talking there to a friend who had been watching the shells falling farther up the town. I was only out about a quarter of an hour, and had just got into the garden, when I heard the Boer cannon fire, and in a few seconds the unmistakable "whiz" of a shell, followed at once by its explosion, let me know that trouble was mighty near. I went out to see where it had burst, and found it was in the main road close by. One piece struck a *Kaffir* woman on the back of the head and knocked her brains out, and she fell on the pavement and died in a few minutes, not a hundred yards from our house in a straight line, in Dutoitspan Road, near the club. Another woman who was walking with her was not touched. Another piece of the shell cut a thickish branch off a tree exactly where I had stood talking to my friend a quarter of an hour before.

This was getting near with a vengeance, and I did not at all like it, as our house stood a good chance of getting hit, being two-storied, while all the others around it were only one story high. However, though they shelled away for two hours in the morning and two more in the afternoon, nobody else was touched, and no other shell came as near as this one.

After this the Boers kept their guns in the same position and fired at us in a half-hearted sort of way every day except Sunday for a whole week; we had shells in town on the 12th, 13th, 14th, 15th, 16th, 17th, and 18th. They generally began soon after daylight, and went on for an hour or two, till they got tired, or possibly till they knocked off for breakfast, and they usually treated us to an hour or two's performance in the afternoon again. During the seven days of active bombardment

35

they fired at least seven hundred shells into the town, and the amount of damage done both to life and property was so small that it would hardly be believed.

The Boers fancy the Lord fights for them. If they knew how little they had hurt us with their shells, I think they would want a new ally, or else think that their old one was helping us.

Besides the *Kaffir* woman, no one was killed, but a Dutchwoman died of fright when a shell burst near her house. A Dutchman, too, was driving a fare in his cab when a shell dropped on his horses, killing one outright and breaking his own arm, but not damaging the fare in the least. Then one morning early I was rung up, and an unmistakable Hebrew voice yelled up my speaking tube: "Come down at once; a shell has went through my arm." I thought he probably hadn't much arm left after this, but found that it was only a splinter of the shell after all. He had been lying in bed, and a shell had dropped through the roof and burst in his room, a small piece of it going through the fleshy part of his arm, without touching the bone. Another man was said to have been grazed by a splinter on the same day, and this is the sum total of the personal damage done by all those shells.

On the other hand the narrow escapes were numerous, and some of them were simply miraculous. One day a shell came into the Queen's Hotel. It just missed the dining-room where quite thirty people were at lunch, and dropped into the pantry adjoining it. As luck would have it, there were no waiters in the pantry just then, but there were two cats, both of which were killed, and the crockery was a good deal smashed. I believe one man stayed to finish his lunch, but all the rest of the folk lost their appetites and cleared out.

On another day the shells were falling near the house of an old chap (a patient of mine), and he and his daughters went to the front door to look out and see what was happening.

A shell came through the end of the house, across one room, through the wall, across the passage, through another wall and into the bowels of a piano, which was standing up against the wall. There it burst, and a jolly old mess it made of that piano, too. It crossed the passage within eight feet of the people, and not one of them was even scratched, but the piano is only fit for the scrap heap. Another shell came through a roof into a room adjoining a bedroom where a patient of mine was lying ill, and exploded, but did not hurt the patient. I have a piece of this one to make a brooch for Agnes.

One shell fell in an office on to a chair where a man had been sitting writing not a minute before, but who had got up to get something he wanted from another room. Another fell in Dr. Mathias's front garden, just in front of a window, as he and two other men were having lunch just inside (this is the doctor who has the honour of being dear Maria's employer); nobody was hurt, but we hoped that Maria was scared. Another fell on the footpath in front of a tobacconist's shop in the main street, at a most frequented corner, and burst without even breaking the window. Another went through the English church. Another wrecked a small house where one of the club waiters lived, but as the house was in a rather hot corner for shells, he had removed his family and furniture only the day before.

All the time this shelling was going on It was rather nervous work seeing one's patients in the part of the town where the shells were falling. Most of them came from the same direction, and if you were on foot when a gun went off, you had plenty of time and knew just where to shelter; but driving about was different, as you did not hear the gun, the rattle of the cart deadening the sound.

One day I was coming across the Market Square when they were firing, and I suddenly saw a puff of smoke and a cloud of dust in the middle of the street, about one hundred yards in front of me, and there a shell had burst. As several had landed in the same neighbourhood, I turned up a side street, as it was not good enough to get my head caved in. Dr. Symonds had a very narrow escape, as a shell landed and burst within ten yards of his horses' heads.

Lots of shells fell in our forts, but we put up shellproof shelters in them, and not a man was touched. Eighteen fell into one little fort in one afternoon.

Our men got quite expert in dodging the shells. You heard the gun boom, and a few seconds after the "whiz" of the shell came, and you ducked close under a wall or earthbank or shelter of any sort that was handy, and then the shell burst; immediately everyone in the neighbourhood tore frantically towards it to pick up the pieces, for which there was a ready sale, and good pieces, such as the bottom or the conical point with the brass fuse in it, would fetch from one to two pounds. It was really laughable to see the shell hunters on the lookout when the firing was hot, and tearing up to the place where the shells burst to collar the bits. In more than one instance lawsuits were threatened over the ownership of pieces of a shell.

Finding how little damage was done, we soon began to treat the bombardment with calm indifference, and the hottest day's shelling did not create a quarter the alarm that the hooters used to do. We became quite learned in shells, too, and talked glibly of shrapnel and ring shells, and time fuses and percussion fuses, and all the rest of it.

The one they were most liberal with, and which we got to know best, was the ring or segment shell. This was about seven inches high, three inches in diameter, and bluntly conical in shape. It consisted of a pile of rings like cogwheels, but with a large space in the centre, and the cogs only held together by very narrow bridges of iron. They are made of very brittle cast iron, and piled one on top of another to the required height, the top ones getting gradually smaller to give the necessary conical shape. Round this pile a thin coating of iron is cast, and then the incomplete shell is smoothed off in a lathe, leaving a smooth, thin coat of cast iron holding the cogs in position.

The hollow in the centre of the cogwheels is then filled with gunpowder, and just before it is fired the fuse is screwed into the point. It is a brass tube about three inches long, and about as thick as an ordinary candle. Inside it is a percussion cap, with a spike so arranged that it fires the cap when the nose of the shell butts up against anything hard. There are two copper bands round the shell. The one near the base is corrugated when it reaches us, but this is due to the rifling in the cannon; the other one is quite plain. These bands fit themselves to the grooves in the gun, being soft metal, and do not damage it as the iron would do. The corrugated one is the one to make brooches out of.

When the shell bursts, the cogwheels are supposed to split up into the separate cogs, and these should, in theory, "spread death and destruction on all sides." As practised by the Boers, however, they seem to be a particularly harmless sort of firework. Our artillery officers tell us this is because the Boers are using their guns at the extreme range to which they will carry, and that if they used them at two-thirds the distance, we should be anything but amused by them. The powder inside the shell is only enough to burst the case, but not to hurl the fragments apart with any degree of force. If, however, the shell bursts whilst it has still a big velocity, the pieces go on with the same velocity, and are very dangerous.

Shrapnel is designed on this plan. The shell does not have to butt up against anything, but is arranged to burst in the middle of its flight, and instead of cogwheels it contains several hundred bullets which scatter, and really do manage the death-and-destruction business very satisfactorily. But these shells are very much heavier than the other

BOER SHELL – NINE-POUNDER

kind, on account of the bullets, and so will only travel about half the distance that the others do; therefore, though a few were fired when our men were out near the Boers, I don't think any ever reached the town.

All this time you have probably been asking yourselves what our men were doing whilst this shelling performance was going on; and there is only one answer to this—*viz.*, cursing the Government.

When first there was any rumour of trouble with the Transvaal, they persistently denied that anything of the kind was possible, and all through steadily refused to let guns or police, or ammunition or soldiers, come up to Kimberley. In fact, they hindered any defence preparations in every way they could. As a result, our regular soldiers are less than six hundred in number, and the best guns we have are seven-pounders—*i.e.*, the weight of the shell they throw is seven pounds.

The Boers have all sorts of guns, even up to one hundred-pounders, though the largest they have used against Kimberley has been a twelve-pounder. The range of the gun increases with the weight of the projectile, and so the result was that the Boers could place their guns well out of the reach of ours, and pump shells into us with perfect safety. Our men were too few to sally out and take their guns, but whenever our guns managed to get within range of the Boers, their firing was splendid—far and away more accurate than those of the Boers—and the Boers did not like it at all. It we had had two fifteen-pounders, not a shell would have ever come into the town, and if we had had two thousand men instead of seven hundred, no siege would have ever taken place.

I think I have nearly told you everything of interest about the shelling. No there is one other matter. All the bombardment of the town came from the north-west, and the people who lived in that quarter were advised to come into the town out of reach of the shells. So they did, and a rough time they had. They took up their quarters in schools and halls and other available places, and were overcrowded and generally uncomfortable. After a week of it they decided that the comforts of their own homes, even with the risk of shells thrown in, were preferable, and so all of them, except a few of the most nervous, went back.

To be safe, they dug pits in their gardens or back yards, and roofed them with firewood or old iron, and put a couple of layers of bags full of earth on top, and then piled loose earth on the top of these, so that when any shelling began they could take shelter in the pit and be safe. Heaps of people had to turn out of their homes on account of the siege, as they lived outside the line of forts, and so were liable to be shot by our own people, as well as by the Dutch in case of attack, and also to be rushed and looted at any time, even when there was no big attack.

All the Kenilworth people came into town quite early in the siege, and are still unable to go home. Then the natives who lived in two of the locations were turned out and sent to a place within the forts, as their huts were liable to give cover to an attacking force. As soon as they were cleared out, the huts were all flattened out and destroyed.

In several instances good houses were razed to the ground for the same reason, and in front of one commanding fort all the garden fences, etc., that ran crossway on were laid down, so that the Boers could not dodge behind them in case of attack. So on the whole our people took very thorough precautions when they really did start, but many people say that if the Transvaal had started business a week sooner than they did, they could have taken the town with the greatest of ease. I think a month sooner they would have done, but not a week.

All this has really brought me no further than November nth, the day on which the bombardment started. On that day our men (the mounted ones, for infantry are no use against mounted Boers) went out and had a brush with the enemy. One of ours was killed, and from subsequent native reports we think several Boers were slain. But our men were at a disadvantage, as they always were in these sorties, for all round the town the bush had been cleared and the Boers could see them coming, and take cover and wait till they got within range, and then blaze away. If they could have plucked up courage to attack the town, our men would have been under cover and the Boers in the open, but that is not the sort of game they care for. As one old Dutchwoman said to me, "The Dutch are very determined."

"Very determined not to get hurt, I suppose you mean," was my answer.

None of us liked these sorties, as they exposed our men too much, but the Boers would not give us a chance to get at them, so we had to make a chance now and then to prevent them getting too cheeky.

Nothing else happened until the 14th, when there were rumours of an ultimatum from the Boer commandant to Colonel Kekewich, giving him twenty-four hours in which to surrender the town, or he would bombard it. At the time we hardly believed this, but later on it turned out to have been quite true, as in a Dutch paper which came

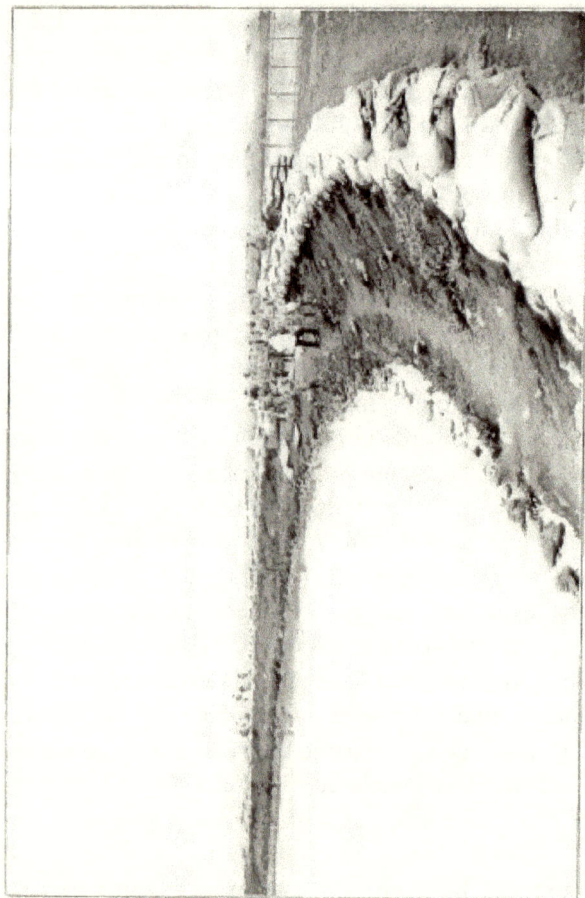

THE RESERVOIR

off one of the prisoners whom our men took one day later on, there was the full text of the commandant's letter and Kekewich's reply. The latter was to the effect that if the commandant wanted Kimberley, he had better come and take it, and further, that as the Boers had been using the white flag for improper purposes, if any one came fooling around with a white flag in future, he would probably get hurt, as all the officers had orders to fire on all white flags now.

This was because the Boers, with their usual deceit, had been using the white flag to get into better cover, and to take other unfair advantage of us. In the first fight they sent a white flag out, and when one of our men went out to it to parley, the Dutchman asked how many men there were out on our side, were they police, or Volunteers, or Regulars, and many such impertinent questions. Naturally our man told him to go to the devil and find out, but the Dutch took advantage of the parley to take up a better position.

Again, when our ambulance waggons were out bringing in the wounded at any of the fights, I think I am correct in stating that the Boers invariably fired at them when they were within range, though each waggon carried a big red-cross flag. And these are the gentle and inoffensive people that Olive Schreiner prates about! Brutes! They are not even decent savages, but just a cross between a bushman and a baboon, only more ignorant than either of their parents.

On the 16th our men had another brush just out to the north-west, one of them being killed and eight wounded. I only got one of the wounded this time, as it was early in the morning, and the message to fetch me got muddled somehow, so I was a little late at the hospital. My man had four holes in him, all from one bullet. It went through the outer side of his left thigh and through his left hand too, which was resting on his thigh at the time, but only one of the small bones of his hand was broken, so he was soon all right again.

On the 17th I had rather a slack afternoon, so we got Dr. Stoney to show us over the forts (to which he was doctor) up at the waterworks reservoir. When we went out, the shells were dropping at the reservoir, so we got on to the *veldt* to one side of it, and looked on a long way off at a brush which was going on in another direction. Our men were out and trying to draw the Boers; but they, as usual, did not see it. Our seven-pounders were on a *débris* heap, and were firing over the heads of our men at the Boers, who were far away hidden in a watercourse.

The rifle firing was tremendous—almost entirely from the Boers, as we learnt later—and it sounded as if about ten waggon-loads of

ROYAL ARTILLERY IN ACTION AT THE RESERVOIR

wounded would be the result, but it wasn't. Only one of our men was hit in the calf of the leg—not a serious wound. Whether any Dutch were potted, we did not know—in fact, that was a thing we never did know. The Dutch paper I spoke of just now gave full accounts of several of these skirmishes, and generally said: "Our loss was one man slightly wounded, but the English suffered tremendously." Then in an out-of-the-way corner you saw: "Franz de Beer, who was killed in the fight at Kimberley on such a date, was the son of so-and-so." This occurred more than once in the same paper. Certainly the Boers were smart in getting away their killed and wounded, but of course they were in their own lines, as they did not advance to meet us as a rule, but let us go to them, which is part of the usual Boer tactics, and they don't ask for anything better. They say, too, that the Boers remove their dead so rapidly by the primitive and crude method of putting a rope round them and yanking them off at a gallop behind a horse.

After watching the fight I have been speaking of, we went on to the reservoir, as the firing had ceased. We saw the guns and shells, and the officer in charge explained them to us. There has been more firing at the reservoir than at any other place, either because the Boers want to pot our guns and disable them or to burst the reservoir bank and let out the water. Lots of shells have plumped harmlessly into the water and some struck the bank, but nobody was hurt. The guns are intact, and the reservoir is as it was.

We don't think much of the Boers as artillerymen, I think I told you that my driver wanted me to buy a house for him some while back. The house he fancied—and which I should have bought, but for a disagreement as to price—is a little way from the reservoir and in the direct line of fire of the Boer guns. No less than three shells went through that house, and several others fell near it. Daniel is now rather pleased that I did not buy that house. I have the entire top, with fuse complete, of one of the shells that fell near it, and a similar one split in halves that fell in Kenilworth. I am going to have them fixed up as paper-weights when we get out of this.

CHAPTER 4

"With C. J. Rhodes's Compliments"

About this time the De Beers Company began to turn its attention to the making of shells. We had a very good supply, but not knowing how long we were going to be shut up, the Company thought they might as well be making some, so they turned to and started, and very well they succeeded. Their shells, though perhaps not so nicely finished as those turned out at Woolwich, gave every satisfaction to our artillery officers, and we trust to the Dutch too; and they had the additional advantage of having "With C. J. R.'s Comps." stamped upon them, which must have mightily amused any gentle Boer who got hit by one. The Company turned out about sixty a day, so we had no fear that shells would run short.

Ever since we were shut in, we have been hearing all sorts of rumours as to the date when our relief column would arrive; even after three days we had "reliable" news that it was at Modder River, and as time went on these got more and more inaccurate. Every one you came across had definite information as to the date when it would arrive, and every one's date was different. At last we came to the conclusion that we would expect it when we saw it.

Things went jogging along quietly without much happening. Most days there was a little shooting between our patrols and the Boers, generally without any damage being done, and most days a few shells were fired either at the people guarding our cattle or at Wesselton or somewhere else. Shells we had got used to, and did not much mind, but on some days when the wind was in the right quarter the report of the gun and "whiz" of the shell sounded very close.

Our bedroom faced the quarter from which most of the shells came, and sometimes when the guns woke me up and sounded very close I used to think they were too near to be pleasant. Downstairs in the hall, even if a shell had come into the house, I hardly think it would have touched us, as it would have had to come through two good brick walls, and I don't think they could do that at the range they were firing at.

On the 24th Agnes and I had quite a nice little excitement. I heard from Mackenzie that the men in one or two of the forts were rather short of tobacco. Many of the better-known forts were loaded up with all sorts of presents from the townspeople, but the more out-of-the-way ones did not come off so well. I laid in twenty pounds of Transvaal tobacco and two hundred cigars, and went round to the neglected forts. At one of them that looked north we had quite a bit of fun. The men were very polite and showed us everything—a Maxim gun, amongst others, and the man in charge showed us the way it worked. We had some field-glasses with us, and could see the Boers moving around the *veldt* about a mile and three-quarters away, between their head camp and the railway.

Presently the armoured train went out, and the Boers fired a gun at it. The gun was about the same distance from us as from the railway, and they fired across us, so we could see the shots well. They fired six shots at the train, but only one went near it, and then they fired a last shot, and this time they had slewed the gun round and fired at our fort. Of course it was too far off for us to see how the gun pointed, but we saw the flash and puff of smoke, and heard the "whiz" of the shell, evidently coming our way. We did not have much time to think, but the men all yelled to us to crouch down behind the rampart, and the shell struck and burst about a hundred yards away, of course quite harmlessly. Then a message came from the conning tower that everyone was to leave the fort except those actually on duty, so we had to go.

Later on in the afternoon I went up to the top of the conning tower and had a look round. There is a splendid view all over from there, but I only had a few minutes to spare, and you want to be up there hours to take in all the country round, things look so different from the top side. When the trouble is over I will go up and spend an afternoon there with a glass, and take in everything quietly.

On the next morning (November 25th) we were waked about five o'clock by heavy gun firing, and soon after heavy rifle firing began, so I knew there would soon be some wounded about. I got up and went down to the hospital about six, and Watkins turned up soon after. We waited about a little, and then, as there was no news of any wounded, were just going off to a bit of high ground near the hospital to see if we could discover what was going on.

Just then a telephone message came to say that we were to go out where the fighting was going on, as more doctors were wanted. It did not seem the right order, as we knew that there would be wounded coming in presently, and our allotted post was at the hospital; however, it was an order, so off we went. Watkins had a "bike," but mine was busted, and I was walking. I walked along home without meeting a cab, and then I got hold of a milkcart, which took me about a quarter of a mile, and then I found a cab. I went out as hard as I could go, and followed an ambulance that I could see in front of me. We got a little way beyond the barrier when I met some of our men coming in with about a score of Dutch prisoners, and a dirty, low-class-looking lot they were.

A little farther on I met some more of them, and the men who were bringing them in told me the Boers would pot me if I went farther out. However, the ambulance was still ahead, so on I went after it. The rifle firing had been getting a good deal slacker, and by the time I caught the ambulance it had practically stopped. Three or four ambulances were just starting for the hospital, and everyone seemed to have been attended to, but they brought a Boer along with a big hole in his head, and I bandaged him up and sent him along in one of them. The ambulances were on the road just under the crest of a hill, and a good lot of our men were scattered on both sides of the road, also under the brow of the hill. Dr. Watkins was somewhere about. I saw his bicycle on the roadside, but could not see him.

After waiting for a little time, an order came from the colonel that our ambulance was to move off to the left, keeping under cover of the hill, so we went along over the *veldt* for a few hundred yards, and then pretty smart rifle firing began again at the men near whom we were. Then we got an order to draw off home with the ambulance, as our men were going to retire. This being the case, I did not see that I was doing any good there, and I knew that a lot of wounded had gone along to the hospital, and there was only the junior house-surgeon there to receive them, Russell having gone out with the Army doctor to see the fun. So I decided to get back to the hospital as soon as I could.

I took a beeline across the open to my cab, and, as the firing was fairly hot, was a little exposed to it. Five or six bullets whistled over me, probably not aimed at me at all, but I have no doubt they would have laid me out quite as neatly, if they had hit me in the right spot, as if they had been meant for me.

The small-bore bullet makes a tiny little "whiz," more like a big mosquito than anything else, and does not sound as if it could possibly hurt.

I got back to the cab all right, and went straight along to the hospital, and found, as I had expected, heaps of wounded, and no one to look after them. I waded right into them, and Watkins and some more of the doctors soon turned up, so we got them shipshape before long. I got some badly wounded this time. One poor youngster of eighteen was shot in the abdomen, and his bowel was cut open about ten times. I had to cut one piece about ten inches long clean out, and to stitch up a lot of other places; but I felt that he had no chance, and sent for his people and told them so at once. He died about six hours after. His father and mother had cleared out when the war scare began, but he would not go; he stayed and joined the Light Horse. Another man fell to me with a badly broken arm, the bone being very much shattered; and another with a bullet clean through his liver. Another had a bullet in his thigh, which I cut out and have stuck to, together with a big bullet I picked up on the *veldt*. Our loss was six killed and twenty-nine wounded, but we believe that the Boers lost very heavily, and we took thirty-five prisoners.

I forgot to say that two severely wounded Boers fell to me at the hospital. Both of them were rather badly hit, but they did well, and were not long about it. As soon as they were able to get up, I had them transferred to the gaol hospital, as they could easily escape from the big hospital. The man whose head I bandaged up on the field was badly damaged—in fact, Shields said that when he took off my bandage, about a third of the man's brains fell out, and this is very nearly the absolute truth. Anyhow, he lived three days, and would probably have lived altogether, but they washed him, and, being a Boer, the shock to his system was so great that he succumbed.

The history of the day's fight was that our men drove the Boers out of the ridge from which they had been shelling the town with heavy loss, but as strong reinforcements of Boers came up, they very wisely retired, and did not attempt to hold the position.

Watkins got out a few minutes before I did, and was right up in the firing line whilst the fire was still very hot, but he came out all right. Some well-known men were hit in this fight. One poor chap (he is one of the three men who rent my old house) got the middle part of his lower jaw smashed into splinters. It is a horrid wound, not danger-

BOSMAN'S COMMANDO – BLOEMHOF NEAR CHRISTIANA

ous to life, but I am afraid the deformity that is left will be very bad.

Most of the Boer prisoners were of the very lowest class, and came from Bloemhof, a little Transvaal town not far from Christiana, where I have been several times. Two at least of them came from Barkly West, where they had been working in some relief work that the Government had started for the benefit of poor whites. But this is Boer gratitude. Some of these prisoners had Free State newspapers on them, which gave us later news than any we had been able to get.

These papers gave a letter from the commandant who was bombarding Kimberley, in which he said he had directed his shells to the middle of the town to "do as much damage as possible." This, like firing on ambulances, is directly against the Geneva Convention, which lays down that bombardment should, as far as possible, be directed against fortifications, and not against private buildings. But the Boer cares for none of these things; he is just an ignorant savage, and knows and cares nothing for conventions.

On the whole this was a good day's work, though we lost rather heavily; but it showed that the Boers were not always invincible, even behind their earthworks.

The next day a doctor came in from the Boers for chloroform and brandy. He was a Scotchman, and said he had been compelled to go with the Boers—which is a little thin, as he could have stayed in Kimberley if he had wanted to when he was here. He got his chloroform and brandy all right.

On the 28th we had another fight. When I came in to lunch I found a note from the captain of the Ambulance Corps asking me to be ready to go out with the ambulance at 3.30 p.m., as our men were going out in force. I wrote a note to say all right, but ran across the man who he said had told him to write to me. In the course of conversation I said that I should be there to time, and he asked me what I meant. When I explained, he was surprised, and said I must stay at the hospital and not go out, as he had got a wigging for sending Dr. Watkins and me away from our posts a few days before. I was a bit disappointed, but of course had to obey orders; and, as it turned out, I did not miss much. All the afternoon there was lots of firing, both rifle and artillery, but no wounded turned up. About half-past seven we got news that the wounded were coming in, so I went down to the hospital.

Dr. Mackenzie had been somewhere watching the fight, and came in with glowing accounts of the way in which our men had hammered the Boers, stormed their fort, taken their big gun, and generally done great things. This was very nice, but when the wounded turned up we began to hear another tale. The first few said that we had lost heavily, but knew no details; and then others came who told us that Colonel Scott Turner, who commanded all the mounted men, was killed, and lots of others, and that we had not taken the gun, or fort, or anything else.

The wounded kept straggling in by ones and twos, and now and then an ambulance brought more, and so it went on until about 2.30 a.m., when the last one was finished. Altogether about thirty wounded were treated, but I only got about six of them, for, after doing a few, Watkins got a man who was shot through the bowels, and he asked me to help fix him up. It was a worse mess than I had had with my own man a few days previously, and took nearly two hours to fix up. The poor chap only lived about twelve hours after.

We got home to bed about three, and were uncommonly glad to get there. Next day was a very sad one, for by this time we knew that we had lost a lot of men, but how many we did not know till the Boers sent in to say they had nineteen of our dead, and we could fetch them; and so we did. The total loss was twenty-two killed at the time, and two died after in hospital. The nineteen were so smashed up that there was some ground for the rumours that after our men had retired the Boers had gone round and finished off any wounded who were still alive. They had all been very near the Boer fort, so that might account for the severity of their wounds, but nobody knows except the Boers.

The colonel was shot dead, quite close to the fort, leading on his men. He was a very brave man, but rash, and though the townspeople were a good deal upset at his death, there was a curious undercurrent in his own men's sorrow. They all felt that he was reckless, and likely at any time to endanger all their lives. Of course they all knew that any of their sorties were very risky, but Turner always seemed to go in for unnecessary risks, and the men naturally did not like it.

All the dead were buried on the Wednesday afternoon (November 29th), and the whole town was gloomy. It is said that Scott Turner's orders were to attack the Boer position and do what he could, but not to press the attack on the fort, as that would be too costly; but Turner could not hold himself, and went for the fort.

In one of the Boer positions which our men took they captured one hundred and fifty shells of a very deadly kind, seven barrels of gunpowder, and a few other things; but the price we paid for them was far too heavy. On that same Wednesday night we got signals from the relief column that they were coming along.

From this time things were pretty quiet, and there was no further firing into the town. Most of the Boers were supposed to have gone down to meet the column, but they left enough to prevent our men doing much; though no actual fighting took place until December 9th, when our men went out to the Homestead and had an artillery fight with the Boers at Kamfersdam. There was a lot of firing, but not much damage was done; one of our men only was killed and two wounded, all of these by the bullets from shrapnel shell, which are just like those I used to make with a mould at home.

CHAPTER 5

Military Eccentricities

About this time the military began to worry us with proclamations. First we all had to report how many horses we had, and a few days later there was a notice that horse-owners might use the horse-feed they had, but when that was done none would be issued except for horses used for military operations. Fortunately my stablemen had a fair supply. Then there was a trouble about condensed milk. None was allowed to be sold except on a doctor's order, and then only for infants and sick people, and one wrote more orders for milk than for prescriptions about this time.

We had been for some time on an allowance of meat. At first it was not very strictly adhered to, but now it began to be doled out in the regulation quantity. We were very lucky, for our butcher used to send us ours the same as usual; but he was the only butcher allowed to have meat by the military, and most people had to go and wait their turn and scramble for the meat. As most of the men in town were in the Town Guard, in many cases the women had to go and try to get the meat allowance for themselves, and were often shoved out of the way and did not get any. There was a great deal of growling about the meat supply, and as there were lots of cattle, it seemed as if a better allowance could be made and a better system of distributing it arranged. Of course I suppose the military officers did their best to arrange these things, and as there were not many of them, they had their hands very full.

As time went on, however, a lot of dissatisfaction arose in the town as to the way the officers went on their way rejoicing and issuing orders that were very nice from their point of view, but did not seem at all calculated to promote the welfare of the townspeople. And a military officer is like a mule—he is so puffed up with his own importance that he never listens to any other view of a matter except his own. Personally our officers were very nice people, but as a body I have no doubt their creed was that Kimberley was made for the especial benefit of their regiment.

Well, after this I must get back to the recording of events; but really, except for rumours about the upcoming column, nothing happened until December 9th. On that day our artillery went out to the Homestead and tried to shell the Boers out of a strong position they had taken up in one of the outside mines, Kamfersdam; but though they blazed away merrily at each other for a long time, not such a great deal of damage was done. One of our men was killed and three were slightly wounded. The Boer loss was two killed and a few wounded, but we don't know how many, and we did not drive them from their position.

On Sunday (the 10th) a little distant firing was heard late in the afternoon, and it was reported that a few shells had been seen bursting on the Spytfontein hills, where the Boers were massed in strong force, the shells having evidently been fired by the relief column.

On the next morning heavy cannon firing began before five and kept on till after nine. It was tremendous, and was just like volley firing with cannon. A dozen reports would come in quick succession, the whole of them perhaps in less than a minute, and for about four hours this sort of thing was almost incessant. Some of the shells could be seen bursting in the same *kopjes* as on the previous night, but whether the bulk of the noise was from our guns or the Boers' we did not know. Of course, after all this we were confident that our column would come in in the afternoon, but somehow or other it did not; and though I am now writing on December 16th, and all this took place five days ago within twenty miles of here, you know far more of what happened than I do. As our column has not arrived, we imagine that the Dutch position was too strong for our men to force, but whether this is really so is not known.

We are all mighty sick at the lack of news. Whether the officers have any or not we do not know, but they are very careful that the civilians know nothing. Sixteen days after the fight at Modder River we were allowed to have extracts from the despatches published, and that Is about the time any news is allowed to mellow before we are presented with it. We don't want to know what are the plans of the general, but we can't help wanting to know something of the things that have happened. I suppose the Army red tape forbids anything being told civilians until it is too old to interest them. And the folly of that red tape! Oh, Lord, how silly it is!

The military orders on one occasion towards the end of November contained the interesting information that on *October 6th* a company of the Town Guard went out to the rifle butts to practise, and returned after they had finished. Another day the titbit was that mule No. so-and-so, belonging to the Royal Artillery, had died, and was accordingly struck off the strength of the regiment from the date of its death. Then, again, a few nights ago, when the searchlights were signalling, an important message was sent through, and all concerned strained their eyes to get hold of it rightly. When got it was: "What is the number branded on the hoof of the horse issued to O———?" O——— is the military doctor, and he has not heard the last of that horse yet.

After the heavy cannonading on the 11th, everything was deadly dull for a time. A few distant guns were heard on the 12th, and now and then the Boers dropped a few shells into Wesselton, but beyond this there was no news, and nothing doing outside. Inside there was great excitement, for some- how a rumour got around that a proclamation would be issued to the effect that all women and children, and all men not actually bearing arms or in some other way indispensable to the defence of the town, would be compelled to leave Kimberley as soon as the railway was opened. A notice was printed that free passes on the railway would be given to people not able to pay the fare to wherever they wished to go, and this gave some colour to the compulsory story.

Anyhow, though there was no official notification that any such scheme was contemplated, it was known that such a plan had been debated by the Town Council and the military, and later on that the colonel had received positive orders from headquarters to carry it out. The reason was that as the railway from here to Orange River (eighty miles) ran through what was practically enemy's country, it would need to be guarded all the time, or the Boers would rip it up again. Then to efficiently guard that length of line would need an enormous number of men, for unless almost every yard was looked after carefully, a single Boer could sneak in and take out a rail or two and so disgruntle the line again. As this enormous number of men could not be spared for long, the authorities saw there was a choice of two things—either to bring up food to Kimberley or take Kimberley to the food, and then let the line look after itself.

Naturally, being officials, the wrong thing seemed right to them, and they seem to have decided to take Kimberley to the food. This was very nice in theory, but when you consider that all the colonial towns—Cape Town as well as others—were already overcrowded with refugees from up-country, the hotels and boarding-houses being full up, it seemed to our people that in leaving Kimberley they would just be going from the frying-pan into the fire. Then, again, heaps of people who were struggling along here, and only just able to make ends meet, would be hopelessly ruined by leaving.

The railway notice said that no excess luggage would be taken, and this meant practically that the people would have to go with what they stood in. Oh, it was a foolish notion, and the very mention of compulsion got the people's backs up. Had there been any attempt to carry out the compulsory exodus, I firmly believe there would have been civil war in the town, and that would either have resulted in surrendering it to the Boers or in telling the military to get out and leave us to look after ourselves. One man told the colonel in almost so many words that if our own countrymen were going to turn us out of the homes we had earned and worked for, surrender to the Dutch could not possibly bring anything worse upon us. Anyhow, feeling ran very high, and the whole town was badly upset.

To do our colonel justice, I believe he saw the absurdity of the proposal at once, but he had his orders and could not absolutely go against them, though he did not actually hurry to carry them out. Had he been able to publish a proclamation when the scare began, to the effect that hard times were coming and that it was advisable for all people who were able to do so to leave the town, and that every possible assistance and facility would be given them to do so, but that no one who did not wish to leave would be compelled to go, none of this feeling would have arisen.

I suppose that this would have been too directly flying in the face of the orders of his superiors, and so could not be done. Anyhow, a very strong protest was sent off by Rhodes and other important people, showing the folly of compelling the people to leave, and for the present the matter stands over till our relief column arrives.

It is pretty generally thought that the wire which Rhodes and some other prominent men sent off some weeks ago, urging that immediate relief must be sent to us, caused the issue of the compulsory departure order, the authorities at the Cape or at home thinking the matter to be more pressing than it really was.

At present, however much any one wants to get away, there is no communication, so it can't be done. All the week (December nth to 17th), we have been longing to hear some news of the column's advancing, but not a syllable of news have we heard. Rumours are around in plenty, the favourite one being that as the Boers hold a very strong position in the Spytfontein *kopjes*, through which the railway comes, and our men failed to shell them out, it is said that the next move is to try and surround them in the *kopjes*, and cut off their food and water supply, at the same time bringing the railway round the *kopjes*, either on one side or the other, in spite of the Boers.

It sounds all right, and the country to the east of the *kopjes* is pretty flat for a railway, and has no very steep gradients; but it is rather a big order, and would apparently take a long time. Today (December 18th) we had news in the paper of the big fight on the nth at Spytfontein, and our guesses were not far out. There was a heavy engagement there, and we lost severely, as any attacking force must always do when advancing in the open against a strongly entrenched enemy. The column did not succeed in turning out the Boers, but inflicted a heavy loss upon them, possibly heavier than our own, but of that we cannot be sure. However, an irregular force feels the loss of its men far more than a regular one, especially a Boer force, for they are as a rule mighty frightened of getting hurt. We hope, therefore, that the Boer loss has been great enough to discourage them a little, but this we shall find out later.

Whenever we have had a little time all through the siege, we have wondered how Mafeking was getting on. We have had news at long intervals, and generally much to the same effect—*viz.*, that heavy bombardment is still going on. It is simply wonderful how that little place has held out, and we would give anything to help them to hold out until they are relieved. If they are able to do so, I think their defence will be one of the pluckiest in history. They have been shelled almost the whole of the siege, and our shelling has been the merest child's play to theirs. The Boers have never used anything heavier than a twelve-pounder against us so far, while at Mafeking they have used forty, sixty, and even a hundred-pounder, and yet those chaps hang on and keep getting a few Boers here and there when they have a chance, and simply will not give in. Fortunately they were well supplied with food at the beginning, and got most of their women and children out.

December 24th.—All the last week things have been quiet. Our men have been out a few times, and a little shooting has been done on both sides, but we have had no one hit, and I don't expect they have either. The Boers are leaving us alone, and both sides are just waiting. Our men cannot advance on the Boers, as their position in the *kopjes* at Spytfontein is too strong, and the Boers cannot leave Spytfontein without letting the relief column get into Kimberley, so they are apparently just sitting looking at each other—at any rate, as far as we know. In the meantime the Boers are leaving us in Kimberley quite alone, and are even dismantling the forts from which they shelled us earlier on, probably taking the sandbags to fortify other positions from which to harass the column.

Our Kimberley men are quietly doing all they can to prevent the Boers being comfortable in these positions again by filling up the wells and cutting the dams; so that if they do come there again, their water supply will be a difficulty to them. We hear now that the Spytfontein lot are rather in difficulties for water, and that is quite likely. We hear, too, that typhoid and dysentery are playing them up, which is more than likely, for the average Boer is a filthy beast, and has less idea of sanitation and cleanliness than the domestic barn-door hog. We are getting quite our share of these troubles, in spite of all our care, and the Dutch must be having a warm time with them.

On the 21st we had another sad mishap. A corporal in the Mounted Police, after going round and inspecting his outlying pickets, went off towards the Boer lines without saying anything to his men. They did not see him go, and consequently when they saw a man some four or five hundred yards away spying and scouting about, they fired at and killed him. It was just getting dark, and he had not said a word to anyone about going, so no blame could possibly be attached to the men. It was absolutely his own fault, but it is very sad to kill one's own men all the same. There is no doubt that a man who was shot earlier on in the siege in a mysterious manner when out scouting was killed in the same way by his own men.

We have not had any cheerful news about our forces down the colony and in Natal this week—in fact, they all seem to be making a mess of it. To the non-military man who knows something of the country, all three columns seem to be running their heads against stone walls when they try to turn the Boers out of the hills in Natal, at Stormberg, and at Nauwpoort. Many of these hills are almost unscalable, and to try and take them in face of a strong force armed with magazine long-range rifles seems the height of folly.

The plan that commends itself to the common-sense civilian mind is to keep a sufficient force at these hilly places to prevent the Dutch advancing into the colony, and then to send a column into the Free State through the flat country anywhere between here and Orange River. However, I hope those in charge of the Army really do know what they are about, but at present it seems as if, when they had spelt "South Africa," they had come to the end of their knowledge.

We have now been cut off for ten weeks, and seem just as near relief as we were at the beginning. Personally I have not felt the nip much yet, if at all, because I have a good balance at the bank, and all our tradespeople know that we are good payers, so we get things often when other folks don't. Soon after the siege began we started quietly getting in stores, and we are pretty well supplied, so that I think we could last out a month quite comfortably, and six weeks by spinning things out, even if we could not buy a thing in town, but the bulk of the people are nothing like so well off. Many of them got in lots of stuff, but began to use it directly the siege began, which is the worst sort of foolishness. So far we have not touched any of our reserve, and keep adding to it little by little as we can. There is some talk to the effect that we may be required to hang on till the end of January, and for all one can see, that is the earliest date we shall get free, so once again I will remark, Damn the Government!

It is beginning to be very hard now for infants and invalids, as there is very little food to be got of the sort they ought to have. Most of the milk-farms just outside the town have been looted and the cattle driven off by the Boers, so that there is hardly any fresh milk to be had, and there is no great stock of condensed on hand. The military people are husbanding the latter as carefully as they can, but I don't see how it can last very long. No one can buy a tin of milk without a doctor's order, and this has to be countersigned by the military officer in charge of all stores. Most of us doctors are careful to give orders only to proper cases, but I am afraid that others give them indiscriminately.

All this time work has been pretty brisk. Dr. Fuller got cut off, as I have previously told you, and I have a few of his best patients, and besides this, there is a lot of sickness about. The men kept moderately well because most of them are in the Town Guard out in the forts, and so they get more fresh air and less whiskey than usual, but a good many get fever or diarrhoea or dysentery, the last two from the coarse food and the quantity of water they drink, on the hot days. This makes a lot of work, but not paying work.

Quite early Mackenzie and I decided that we should treat all members of the defensive forces free, unless their illness was due to drink or other foolishness. It did not seem fair to charge these men, many of whom actually were risking, and all of whom might have to risk, their lives in the defence of the town and us, and though I think we were the first to start this, all the other doctors quickly fell into the same way. But there was lots of paying work, too, amongst the women and children, the latter especially giving us a bad time. At the best, young children die here with great rapidity in the hot weather; and the upside-down state of affairs of course makes things worse than usual this year. Then, too, quite half one's patients go off to the sea for December and January, and they can't get away this year.

So on the whole the amount or paying work has been a good deal larger than usual this season. But we don't get much money in, all the same, for several reasons. First of all, Dorward, our collector, is in the Town Guard, and gets very little time off, and then we have told him only to send accounts out to the people who can well afford to pay. Even if he were at liberty as much as usual, we should not let him go round collecting as he usually does. The folks have too much on their hands to be worried for doctors' money just at present. As long as we can make enough to live on, we shall be satisfied for the present.

December 26th.—Christmas over once more, and relief as far off as ever. Early on in the siege, the folks who wanted to be really funny talked about relief reaching us about Christmas-time, and we all thought this was a joke, but the jocular part does not seem quite so excruciatingly funny now. Christmas Day was very quiet, even more so than the one I spent on the North Sea. There we had sufficient excitement when we found that the leg of pork we had been saving for Christmas had gone bad, but even that was denied us here. We did not expect our ducks, for which we paid a pound, to be anything much, and they weren't. We had Dr. Stoney and his brother to dinner, and I think they enjoyed themselves in a quiet way.

There had been rumours that a great fight was going to take place again at Spytfontein, but nothing happened. Today there have been rumours that Plumer has got down from Bulawayo and relieved Mafeking, but that is much too good to believe until properly confirmed. There have been rumours of another sort for the last few days—*viz.*, that the Boers have captured a train full of lyddite and other ammunition somewhere between Orange River and Spytfontein, and this is so bad that it probably is true. We have no doubt that the Boers will get hammered in the end, but at present most of the signs point the other way.

We here in Kimberley are hoping a good deal from Sir Charles Warren. He has been up this way before, and knows both the country and the Boers, but whether he will come or not is very doubtful. There are many men here who served with him before, and they have great belief in him.

We had a Christmas message from Sir Alfred Milner. He did not wish us a merry Christmas, but a lucky one, and we appreciated the wording of the message.

Yesterday we had a new proclamation, to the effect that no one should kill or cause to be killed any ox, cow, bull, sheep, lamb, goat, kid, or pig without permission. So things are getting rather tight. Our nextdoor neighbour has a small red pig (looks like a Tamworth) about six weeks old, that runs about his yard. It seems too funny that he should not be able to kill this small swine without getting a permit. I suppose the idea is that people who kill at home will not be allowed meat from the butcher till they have eaten their kill.

The Boers have been shelling at Wesselton Mine again today, but I don't think they have done any damage. It must be an awful sell to them to find that we have managed a decent water supply after they cut us off from the river. Of course they know about our getting water from Wesselton, and I suppose they keep potting away there in the hope that they may burst up the pumps, but as the machinery is all in the mine, I don't think that they have a very gaudy chance of doing so. However, the more they shoot the better, for modern guns don't stand an unlimited amount of firing, as the rifling wears away, particularly in the heavier ones, so we hope they will pot away (harmlessly) with great vigour.

December 31st.—Very little has happened since I wrote in the way of war. On several occasions we have heard distant firing, so our relief column is either shelling the Boers or being shelled; but which, we don't know. Today there is a rumour that our men have taken Scholtz Nek, which is an important point held by the Boers not far from Spytfontein, but we have not had this confirmed yet.

The paper has been for the last few days full of yarns as to how the War Office and England is wakening up to the fact that they are in for a bigger business than they imagined. This is very reassuring, but one can't help feeling mad at the way we are kept cooped up here, and, as far as we know, no fresh steps at all being taken to help us out. We had hoped that Warren would come up this way, but today I hear he has gone to Natal.

Chapter 6

The Food Problem

Of course we all know that we are merely a pawn in the game, and that it does not much matter to England what becomes of us, but it matters a good deal to us. We are now just going to begin to feel the nip of the siege. One day last week we had a proclamation that various necessaries, such as flour, meal, bread, rice, sugar, etc., would in future only be issued in stated quantities, and that only to the holders of permits. To get a permit for any one of these things you had to make a declaration of the quantities of all of them which you had in your possession, and not only that, but you had also to declare the quantities of every kind of provision which you had. So to get a little, say, sugar, you would have to give the military a list of everything you had, and I have no doubt they would keep a list of those things which you had rather a large quantity of, and commandeer them later on.

This seems all right in theory, but having myself been one of the provident ones, I don't at all appreciate the idea of being looted for the benefit of the improvident ones. The only thing we wanted was bread. We had a good store of flour, but did not care to bake for ourselves if we could help it. I went to Major Gorle, the head of the food supply arrangements, and proposed a compromise to him. My bread allowance came to about twenty pounds a week, so I offered to give his baker twenty-five pounds of flour a week in exchange for that amount of bread, the extra flour to pay for labour and fuel. I thought it seemed a fair offer, but I suppose he thought it would be a bad precedent, for he declined to accept it. He offered, however, to supply me with bread as long as the siege lasted if I handed over all my flour to him in a lump. But this I declined, for he cannot know how long the siege will last, and though my flour would be a drop in the ocean for the whole of Kimberley, it will last me quite three months. So as soon as our baker gives up supplying us with bread, we shall start baking our own.

As for meat, just now we "dunno where we are," for the butcher has given notice that he will not be allowed to supply us after today, as the military are going to take over the meat supply, but so far the military have not made their method of procedure public. Vegetables are also very scarce. The military have taken over the regulation of them, and as usual have so far made a ghastly muddle of it. Yesterday they advertised to supply them at a certain place from 6 a.m. to 10.30. Agnes suggested that she should go and get some, but I, knowing something of the crush there would be, said: "Not much." I went myself at a little after six o'clock, and found the street full, so I came home and did some gardening, and I afterwards heard that nothing was sold till nearly eleven o'clock.

After this I don't look forward with any keen enjoyment to the military administration of the meat supply. We can get a little greenstuff out of our own garden, enough to keep us from getting scurvy, but not much more. When the water was cut off by the Boers, we were not allowed to water our gardens (though many people have done so), and as we imagined a week or two, or at the very outside a month, would see us free, we did not worry about the vegetables, but tried to keep our fruit-trees and vines alive.

Now, however, as we look like being shut up for all time, I am going to run my vegetable-garden again. I have succeeded in getting one of the borough water-carts to bring me two loads of water a week. The water is supplied by De Beers; they have to pump a lot out of the mine, and have laid on a big pipe to the nearest street, and practically any one can get water who cares to lead it. The cart holds' about four hundred gallons, and I have some tanks and barrels to store it in during the days between the loads, so I shall get on all right. Of course the water is very hard, but it is a very great deal better than none,

I have put in potatoes, lettuce, dwarf beans, peas, mustard and cress, and Indian corn this week, and have just got some tomatoes up in the greenhouse to be transplanted presently. Beet is the best thing of all to grow here; it grows well, and you can take the outside leaves off time after time just like we used to do off the wurzels at Garton for the cows. When the leaves are boiled, you can't tell them from spinach.

At last a Dutchman has been decently sentenced for communicating with the Boers. He lived far out at Wesselton, and on two occasions was seen after dark to leave his house (the last one in the village)

and go in the direction of the Boer rifle-pits, not returning for several hours. He could have no possible business in that quarter at that time, so he must have been communicating with the enemy. The judge wanted to give him a year, but the other members of the court declared that they would sit for ever unless the sentence was three years' hard, and so eventually the judge gave way, and he got it.

A Dutch lawyer, a prominent Bondsman who cleared out from here the day before we were cut off was captured by Methuen's people some weeks ago, and is now in gaol at Cape Town. Rumour says that when caught he was in an office telegraphing some information to the Boers, but the truth is not known. Now he keeps writing to his relatives asserting his innocence, and they publish his letters. He says he was arrested by the Boers, as he was suspected by them, and that, being a leading Bondsman, he was suspected by the English, When he is tried, I have very little doubt his Boer friends will swear that he was arrested by them, but Kimberley will never believe that, whatever the court does.

I hear today that the Pretoria Boers are very cocky as to what the end of the war will be. They say that when England sues for peace, their terms will be Natal, Bechuanaland, and Griqualand West to be given up to them, and any other parts of the colony in which the majority of the inhabitants wish to be under the Dutch flag. They will also demand the payment of twenty millions. Fairly good cheek, haven't they?

We hear that Roberts and Kitchener are coming, or, rather, are already on the way, and heaps of troops of all sorts, but it is an anxious time. Try as I will, I don't find I can take my usual amount of interest in the work, and as to settling down to read professional literature, that is quite out of the question.

January 5th, 1900.—Very little has happened in the war line since the last entry. On several days the Boers have fired a few guns at our patrols or the cattle guard, and one shell came into the town and went through an inhabited house two days ago, with the usual result—no one hurt. We hear that the Australian contingent drove the Boers out of Douglas on January 1st, and today there are rumours that they have done the same at Barkly West, but I hardly think this will be confirmed. But if nothing military has been happening, we have had lots of other distractions. On January 1st the new proclamation about meat came out. The butchers had to cease selling at their shops, and the whole arrangement was taken over by the military. The new al-

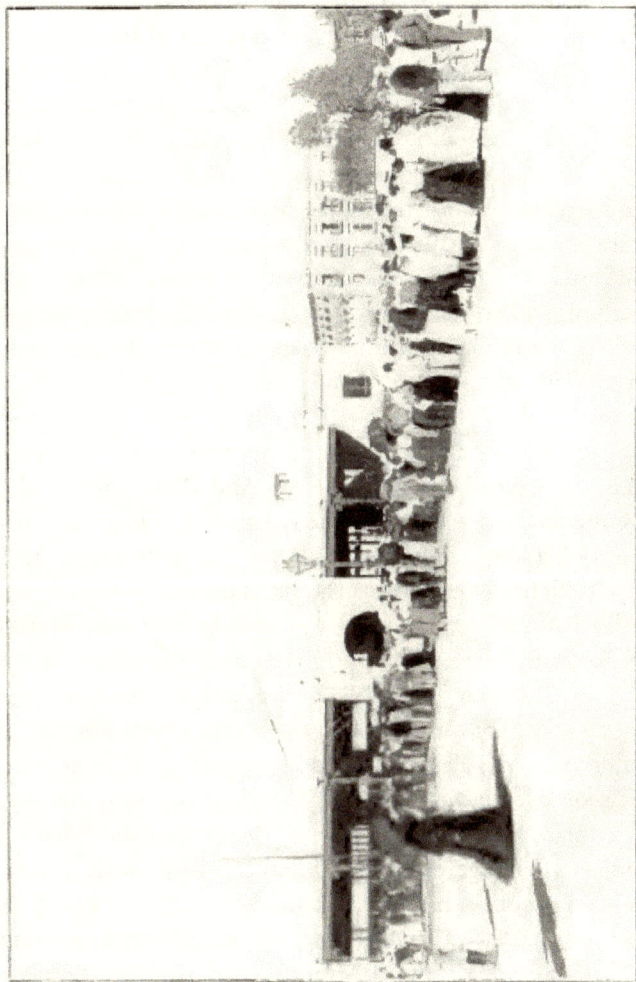

WAITING TURN FOR MEAT ALLOWANCE

lowance was a quarter of a pound per day for adults, and two ounces for children under twelve.

The meat was to be distributed in the new Market Hall, and the three wards that formed half the town were to go in and be served at one side, and the other three on the other. This was for white people only; coloured folks and natives had a separate place, each in a different part of the town. Railings were put up at the sides of the Market Hall, with three gates, and each ward formed up in front of its own gate, in a two-and-two string, and was let in four at a time.

The day before the new arrangement began every head of a house had to send in a notice stating the number of adults and children there were in his family, and the quantity of meat he wished to draw, so that when he turned up for his supply, his demand could be checked from the list made out from all the requisitions. He was then given a numbered card, with the quantity he was entitled to stamped upon it and properly signed, so that in future he would just have to show this card and there would be no further bother. The distribution began at 6 a.m. on the 3rd.

Agnes wanted to go and fetch our supply, but I did not care for her to do so. I had been out in the night and was tired, so we neither of us went that day, as we had enough meat on hand. Being the first day, all the arrangements were strange and the tickets had to be made out and so on, so it took a long while, but it was very superior to the previous indiscriminate fighting for meat at the butchers'.

Next day I went along about 6 a.m. and found I was pretty late, heaps of folks being there before me. I came near the tail of the string. My ward (No. 2) and another (No. 6) are each of them quite three times the size of any of the others, so these wards were not half done when the others were all served, and consequently were at a disadvantage. It took over an hour to draw my pound of meat that day. All dealings are for cash, nine pence a pound being the fixed price.

The officer in charge of all food matters, Major Gorle, is a smart man, and he saw at once that it would not do to put the two big wards in a worse position than the small ones, so for the third morning he arranged that the two big wards should draw two days' supply one day, and on the next day the four small ones should do the same. This hurried things up a good deal, for of course only half the people had to be served every day instead of the whole of them That day I left the house about half-past five, and was back very soon after six. Vegetables are to be given out in a similar way twice a week, but I have not been

68

on a vegetable day yet.

The present arrangement is very good. The elimination of natives and coloured people, and the presence of a few police and soldiers, makes everything quite orderly, and, but for the tediousness of waiting your turn, fairly comfortable. Inside the hall the meat is laid out on the tables ready cut up and weighed into half, one, two, three, four pound lots, so when you show your ticket the man sees in a minute how much you are entitled to and hands it over. There is nothing that a lady need object to in the whole business now, so I shall let Agnes go if I happen to be out on the days we want our supply.

You are allowed to send another white person, servant or otherwise, to fetch your ration, but he or she will have to take his turn just in the same way. You are also allowed to send a coloured or native servant, but these have to wait till the whites present are all served, so that dodge is not good enough, or we should send John. Our white servant is too big a fool to send, so one of us has to go.

It is very funny to see all the town's big swells either fetching their meat themselves or sending a member of their family for it. Parsons, lawyers, doctors, business men, we are all there, and it is a huge joke that we are all in the same boat, but it is to be hoped the joke won't last too long. Previous to this, we have all thought that as long as there was a decent balance at the bank, nothing could go far wrong, but now we find that the balance is of very little use. You can only buy necessaries, and these only in strictly defined quantities, not too liberal. As for luxuries, they are either not to be had at all or else only on production of a medical certificate that they are absolutely necessary, as you are ill. So unless you have a private stock of luxuries, or other things intermediate between necessaries and luxuries, you have to live very sparely and monotonously.

The permit business is a perfect nuisance to us doctors. Every patient you have ever seen, whether sick or not, considers that there are special circumstances which entitle him or her to have a permit from you to buy milk, butter, stout, cheese, oatmeal, mutton (beef or veal only being generally supplied), extract of beef, and heaps of other things. We are between the devil and the deep sea. On the one side the patients clamouring, and getting offended if they don't get permits for everything they fancy, and on the other Major Gorle making trouble if we send in too many. Most of us only give them in cases where we feel sure that the applicant is actually suffering in health for want of the food-stuff asked for; but some of the doctors are either very soft-hearted or easily imposed upon. Milk (condensed) is the chief thing wanted, and the stock is none too great, so we have to be careful.

The Boers have raided most of our milk cows, so fresh milk is very scarce, but there is some, and we are amongst the lucky ones who get it. You would think that the military would have asked the doctors to hold a meeting and decide what to do about permits for milk and other things, giving us a rough idea of the amounts in stock and the daily amount it was safe to issue; but such Is not the military way. So far they have given us no instructions whatever, and within the last three days they have told me that the total available amount per day is twenty tins, Watkins that it is forty, and Mackenzie that it is twenty-five. You can't work with figures like that.

Now the colonel is half inclined to commandeer all the fresh milk and issue it only to infants and invalids. This would be rather a good plan, as it would save a lot of the condensed milk, and we should then have a reserve in case the milk cows had to be killed for food. We should miss our fresh milk, but would quite gladly give it up, if we were sure it fell into the right mouths when we had done so. At present, if we did, it would probably go to someone who needs it no more than we do, and that is not worthwhile. Many of the people are very good about the milk. The De Beers Company supplies the hospital with a great deal, and just now they are sending a good quantity to Agnes for free distribution among the sick and poor. She is a boss in the Benevolent Society, and so knows who is deserving. One patient of mine has a cow of his own, and after keeping a moderate supply for his own children, he allows me to use the rest for anyone who needs it, free.

Everyone, however, is not so good. Some genius who did not care for black tea or coffee struck the happy idea of getting in some of the tinned infants' foods which contained milk and using them as milk. This however, did not last long, as I expect the fact of young single men buying babies' food led to inquiries. Anyhow, one of the parsons told me of it, and I went straight off to Gorle to suggest the commandeering of all infants' foods, and found that he had already done so, so he is pretty wide awake.

Today (January 7th) I got my supply of vegetables at the same time as my supply of meat, and considered myself lucky to get them. The quantity was for half a week for four people, and consisted of a bunch of five carrots, none of them big, four small parsnips, and nine beetroots, none of them as big as a big radish—price one shilling. But one gets a few little presents, or is able to buy small quantities of vegetables and fruit from people who have wells in their gardens, and so are independent of the water supply.

Today Mackenzie bought a lot of beautiful peaches for himself and me at three-halfpence each. Agnes says I am to say that eggs are six shillings and sixpence a dozen. Butter is a thing of the past, except in tins, and that only (as usual) with a doctor's certificate. We had several lots of beautiful fresh butter from a patient long after it was unbuyable. She had a child down with scarlet fever, and consequently was afraid to send the butter to her brother's and sister's families for fear of infecting them, but you bet I did not mind that, and offered to buy her surplus stock. She refused, but gave me about a pound several times. Of course I made it level with honey or sweets, or something of that sort, for the kids.

On January 1st we were delighted to find a notice in the paper that the water would be turned on for watering gardens on and after Tuesday, January 2nd. I found the tap would run on the 1st, so I stole a day and gave all my garden a fine old soaking. Having been so virtuous all those weeks and not used a drop of tap-water unnecessarily, I felt easy in my mind.

Now we thought we should be able to grow all sorts of vegetables, and so we rushed lots of seeds in. I also put in a patch of barley to cut green for my horses, only a little one, but still it will be a help. I put in some *mealies* too, but you will know them better under the name of Indian corn. When they grow up, the green stems and leaves are good fodder for horses. I had a few plants already in of sweet *mealies*, such as the Americans call sweet corn or popcorn, and I stuck a lot more of them in. I got the seed from Gardner Williams, who, you will remember, is the general manager of De Beers, and is an American— and a first-class one too.

But, alas! on Friday a new notice appeared, that no gardens were to be watered, under the same pains and penalties as before. This was bad. But as the taps seemed inclined to run still, I thought it a pity to disappoint them and let them set fast for want of use, so I watered away on the sly, Friday, Saturday, and today (Sunday, January 8th). But I have talked the thing over with one of the waterworks men and the military officer who is responsible for the water supply, and they give very good reasons why the gardens cannot be watered, so I shall relapse into virtue again, and use tap-water only for necessary domestic purposes; but I mean to give up the measly little saucer-bath we have

71

been using, and use my big bath with a fair quantity of water.

The reasons why we can't water our gardens are these: all our water supply now is pumped from Wesselton Mine, and the daily supply is two hundred and fifty thousand gallons, whereas the daily consumption, without watering any gardens, is three hundred thousand gallons. When the water-pipes from the river were cut by the Boers, our reservoir was full, but the difference between supply and consumption lowers it about half an inch a day; so if the siege lasts long enough, the reservoir will in time become empty.

Another reason is that the Dutch are always shelling Wesselton, so one day they may happen to drop a shell into the pump, and then goodbye to our water. The pipes from Wesselton run a good long way outside our line of defences, and the Boers could cut them easily enough if they knew just where they ran, and had the pluck to come and do it.

If either of these things happened, the water in the reservoir would be the last we should get, so it is wise to keep it as full as we can without actually stinting ourselves for necessary water.

When the water was on, we thought we were going to do great things in the gardening line, and grow almost enough vegetables to keep us going. We put a lot of seeds in; but whether we shall manage to keep them going, is another matter. Greenstuff for horses being very scarce, I put in a little patch of barley, and a lot of *mealies* in the trench down which the bath-water runs. The *mealies* when cut green make good food for horses. Of course I shall have nothing like enough to feed them on, but it will give them a taste of greenstuff.

CHAPTER 7

Horse for Dinner

Forage is a big difficulty just now. The military give us doctors a
forage allowance, dry *mealies* principally, but nearly all the cabs have
stopped for want of forage for the horses, and the trams are going to
be stopped next week, I hear. There are no horses for the milk or bread
carts; everybody has to fetch his own. Presently there will be no carts
in the place except the military ones, the doctors', and the hearse.

At last (January 10th) we have begun to feel the siege a little more
acutely. On Monday the people who went for meat were told that
they could only take half their allowance in beef; the other half must
be taken in horseflesh or else gone without. Lots of people went without. We are not compelled to kill horses just yet, but as forage has become so scarce, plenty of horses which are now in fair condition must
be turned out on the *veldt*, and there they will soon become very poor.
The authorities therefore very wisely decided that they had better be
eaten before this happened, and so started to kill them off.

Somehow one does not quite relish the idea of eating horse, but it
must be simply because one has not been used to doing so. The horse
is a clean enough feeder, and ought to be all right. Monday was not
my meat day, but I went along on Tuesday and took my whack of
horseflesh like the rest. By the way, I had managed for the first time
on that day to get a meat ticket which allowed me to go in at the exit
door and get my allowance at once without waiting. I had not before
tried to do so, as I did not want to take an unfair advantage; but I
found that a few people were getting these tickets who had certainly
not such good reasons for wanting them as I had, so I waded in and
got one too. I brought my chunk of horse home, and that night we
had it for dinner. If I had not known what it was, I am sure I should
not have known it from beef. It was tender and good enough for any-

HORSE-MEAT NOTICE

thing, but all the same it took some pushing down, and I did not take a second helping. I guess I am not hungry enough yet.

January 14th.—There is a very good yarn going around about the horseflesh; I don't know whether it is true or not, but it ought to be. Colonel Peakman, who is in command of all the mounted men here— Cape Police, Diamond Fields Horse, and Kimberley Light Horse—is the hero. The first day horse was served out, some of it was cooked for the officers' mess at the mounted camp. At the table Peakman said: "Gentlemen, I am sorry to say that we were unable to get all our ration in beef today and had to take part of it in horseflesh. This which I am carving is beef, the horse is at the other end, and anyone who prefers it can help himself."

Nobody did prefer it, and so they all ate beef and made a good dinner. When they had finished, Peakman suddenly said: "By Jove! gentlemen, I find I have made a mistake in the joints; this is the horse-flesh and the other is the beef." It was just a dodge of his to get them started on the horseflesh. Since writing about our own experience of horseflesh we have had two more lots, both times steak, and this is as good as anyone can want. It does not taste quite like beef, but is very good; even Agnes enjoyed it today.

All the week there has been a little shelling at intervals in the day-time, but nothing much. News of the column is scarce—in fact, we have given up thinking about it, and go along letting the evil of the day be sufficient for it, and you bet it is.

The talk all day is of food, and of the permits necessary to get it. The milk business has changed hands now. I think I told you the colonel was talking of commandeering all the fresh milk for infants

FACSIMILE OF TICKET FOR SOUP

75

and invalids, but he decided not to. Instead he has handed over the administration of the milk to a civil committee consisting of Mr. Judge, the Mayor (Mr. Oliver), Dr. Stoney, Dr. Mackenzie, Dr. Watkins, and myself. How I came to be there I don't know, but there I am.

A central depot has been taken for the issue of the milk, and we have been trying to get people, both dealers and private people, to send their milk to this depot. This has been done by publishing an appeal to all people who are strong and well to give up using milk, so that infants and sick folk may get it. We have given up ours now, and many people have done the same. The milk is served out at the depot, but only to those who have a medical certificate that they require it. The military hand over one case (forty-eight tins) of condensed milk a day to us, and tell us that we need not ask for any more, as we shall not get it. This tinned milk is issued in the same way—only on medical certificates.

After the first day's work we found that the demand so far exceeded the supply that to give everybody a chance we should have to make the quantity issued to each very small, so we cut down the fresh milk to half a bottle a day, and the condensed to one tin a week for each person, irrespective of age or illness or anything. This worked well as far as the fresh milk was concerned, but as one hundred and forty-four applied for tins, our forty-eight did not nearly meet the requirement. Tinned milk is more popular than fresh for several reasons: many babies can't take fresh at all, a tin is supposed to go farther than seven half-bottles, and saves sugar besides, and a tin has only to be fetched once a week, whilst the fresh needs fetching every day.

Of course the quantities are quite insufficient, but we hope to get on better and be able to give larger quantities of fresh milk in a few days' time. The tinned milk problem is hopeless unless we succeed in persuading people who are now getting tins to take fresh milk, and for the reasons above given I don't think there is much hope of that.

Of course the dealers who send in their milk are paid for it, and the people who get orders for it have to pay at a little under the price given to the dealers, but as the De Beers Company sends a big lot of milk free, there is a profit on the whole thing enough for working expenses, and also to allow a certain amount to be given away to poor people who need it.

This is the first time we have been allowed to do anything at all by the military. One day this week I had to write to the colonel about some red-tape difficulties which the Army doctor had put in

76

Order for Milk to be taken to SCHMIDT'S STORE, Market Sq.
Hours : 7 a.m. to 12 noon.

Fresh Milk at 7 a.m.   Condensed Milk at 10 a.m.
(Sundays included)   (except Sundays)

Name *Sarah Jones* .... Age *18 mos*

Address *59 Transvaal Road*

Quantity | Fresh / Condensed | *1 Tin every 5 days*

Length of Time (when possible) *2 Weeks*

Date *12.2.00*

Edmen Ashe

MEDICAL PRACTITIONER.

All orders for Fresh or Condensed Milk must be renewed fortnightly.
Applicant must take a clean jug to the depôt.   Charge 3d. per half-bottle.

FACSIMILE OF ORDER FOR MILK

the way of people getting their food, and I suggested to him very circumspectly that in matters which affected the health and feeding of the people, we all thought that we doctors who knew the town, the climate, and the people might be advantageously consulted. He was very nice, and saw at once that my objection to the red-tape difficulty was sound, and so he altered the routine, but he flatly declined to ask any opinion from the general body of the doctors, as they might have ideas which would "affect the military situation." This is the stock answer to everything.

I believe food (cheese) has been stored until it has gone bad, as if it were issued, it would "affect the military situation." One is often very much tempted to say, "Oh, damn the military situation; let us have a little common sense for a change." The colonel blarneyed me a bit all the same. He said that he should always be glad to talk over medical questions with a single sensible man like myself, but he could not be badgered by all the doctors at once.

Later on in the day he ran across me, and did consult with me over the scurvy amongst the natives. Usually the natives in the compounds get fruit and vegetables enough to prevent their getting scurvy, but since we have had to depend on ourselves for fruit and vegetables the supply has fallen very far short of the demand, and of course the native supply has gone to a large extent to the Europeans. As a consequence, heaps of them have developed scurvy. Nine hundred is the number now on hand.

Gardner Williams had consulted me on the same point earlier in

77

the day. The problem was what we could give the natives, as there was practically no lime juice and no vegetables at all, and they must have vegetable stuff of some kind, or they would all die. I worried over the thing all day, trying to think of something that grew in sufficient quantity and yet was not used by Europeans, and at last I think I struck it.

You have somewhere a small photo, which I sent you when I was at the hospital, of Bishop and myself standing by a clump of those big aloes—they are not really aloes; it is a wrong name, but they are always called so. There are heaps of them all over the town, as they make a very good fence. Now I remembered that in Mexico the natives make a drink of the juice of these things by letting it ferment, so I did not see why the fresh juice should not be used as a vegetable drink for these scurvy boys. And by-and-by I struck a better idea still, and that was to give them the fresh green shoots from the vines. There are many useless shoots on a vine which are cut off to prevent it running too much to wood. When young they are soft and succulent, like the young shoots of a rose-tree, but are refreshingly acid, like sorrel, and I think they should do splendidly. The Company has thousands of vines at Kenilworth, and so they have the medicine (if it turns out to be so) ready to their hands. I told Williams and the colonel these ideas, and they started right away on the vine shoots. The boys like them immensely, and eat them readily. I hope it will be a success, as I shall get some *kudos* if it is, and the natives will get better. The aloe juice will perhaps be tried later, if the supply of the other stuff" should give out.

The native question has been, and is still, a very serious one. At the beginning of the siege we had a good many thousand natives in the compounds—quite fifteen thousand, I should think. Of course these needed an enormous amount of food, and when the siege began to be prolonged, various efforts were made to get rid of them. One big body was sent out early in November, and was promptly sent back by the Boers; but latterly they have been sent out in smaller numbers, and either the Boers are afraid to molest them or they manage to dodge the Boers.

Report says that the Boers are taking them over and either using them to make their entrenchments or to work the mines in Johannesburg. It is rather a sell, if the natives we send out are used to build forts for guns to bombard us; but a native chief I know of here says that the Boers dare not touch his people, as his great chief (Lerothodi, the Basuto head chief) has forty thousand men, well armed, at his command, and would tackle the Free State at once if his subjects were molested.

Perhaps you will wonder why the British don't turn the Basutos on to the Free State. I suppose if the Basutos got the better of the Dutch, they would then tackle the English, for though they like the English much better than the Dutch, if they once got fighting I do not expect they would discriminate between one white and another, especially as they have never been really beaten.

I think there is no doubt the Boers have put up more forts around us, and we are daily expecting more bombarding; this time probably on a larger scale. It has been rumoured all the last week that the new bombardment was to begin next day, but so far it has not commenced. The longer it is put off, the better we shall be pleased, for many reasons. De Beers' are making a big gun, and seem to think that it will be satisfactory; it will carry about a thirty-pound shell, and if anything like successful, should have a range nearly twice that of any gun we have at present. Our gunners seem to be much better shots than the Boers', so we hope they will be able to amuse themselves and instruct the Boers with the new gun, which is expected to be ready in about a week.

One of our men—in fact, he is the builder who built this house— is reported to have done a splendid shot one day last week. The cattle go out a little way to graze, with a strong body of mounted men as a guard, but this guard seems to be placed on the Kimberley side of the cattle. On the other side of the cattle a number of crack rifle shots are scattered behind stones or whatever cover they can get, and they just pot away gently at any Boer within range. The Boers have a similar lot of "snipers" out. Our man is said to have bowled a Boer sniper over at over two thousand yards' range. I hope it is so, for the Boers don't like any other people to do good shooting.

By the way, I think I have forgotten to tell you of our last military order. This came out some time ago, and is that all lights have to be put out at 9.30 p.m. This is to make people careful of their paraffin and candles, whether they like it or not. Of course some permits are allowed, and, equally of course, I have one, as I often read after going to bed. The rule is not rigidly enforced in case of illness, but people have to show evidence that there is illness in the house if so required.

January 21st.—The great event of the week has been the completion and trial of the new gun. Here I was interrupted, and have

79

had no further chance to write until now (January 26th), and in the meantime we have had so much to think about that we have not worried about the big gun. On the morning of Wednesday (the 24th) the Boers began to shell us again quite early in the morning, and we soon found that it was quite different from the shelling we had had before. The shells came from all sides, and, as we found out later, at least eight guns were at work. None of them were bigger than they used before, but they were either better guns or better worked and had better ammunition, for they reached every part of the town, except one small area near the De Beers mine.

January 28th.—Busy again till now. Most of the shells are of the kind we are used to, just like those we had in the first bombardment; but a good many were also the shrapnel, which I told you about before, and which are very much more dangerous. The bombardment went on all the 24th, all that night, and all the 25th until about 9.30 p.m., and then pretty well stopped, though a few shells came in on the 26th, but nothing to hurt. I suppose this even has been child's play to the bombardment of Mafeking, but it has been quite bad enough. During the two days, about eight hundred shells were fired in The hottest time was, as usual, from about 3 a.m. to 8 a.m., and again late in the afternoon, especially down in Beaconsfield at the latter time.

Previously no shells had quite reached us, but they have been all round us this time. We did not bother much about them on Wednesday morning, though we could hear the whiz pretty distinctly and then the report, which showed they were not far away. Just as we were sitting down to breakfast, one whizzed past, apparently very near to the house end, and burst close by, only about a hundred and fifty yards away. Our house is almost directly between the place it dropped and the Dutch gun, so it must have gone very close to us. It was a shrapnel, and it is just as well it missed us.

After this, things quieted down a little, and I don't think any more came quite as close to us. Oh yes, one dropped about a hundred yards from the same end of the house, and wrecked a house just at the back of the military office where all the work is done, but no one was hurt. When I got to the office, at 8.30 a.m., Mackenzie told me he had been fetched out to see a girl who had been killed by one. She had been in one of the shellproof pits, and came out and was dressing in her room, thinking that the danger was over, but a shell came along and burst, and a big piece of it struck her in the back, breaking her spine and almost cutting her in half. Fortunately it killed her instantly. This was the only casualty that day. There were heaps of hairbreadth escapes, but no one else was touched, so far as I know.

One shell went through Rudd's house. He is the son of C. D. Rudd, who has been associated with Rhodes very much in some of his big schemes. He took his family away when war seemed likely, and stored a good deal of his furniture in one room. This was the room into which the shell went, and it made, hay of the furniture. Another went through a patient's house into a bedroom and fell under a baby's cot, but it did not explode. Another exploded under the bed in which was an Indian woman who had been confined only four days. It burst and set the bedding on fire, but did not hurt mother or child; and another came into the same house later in the day without hurting anyone. Another came through the chimney of a patient's house and burst upon the open hearth, and the woman herself in another room did not know about it till a neighbour came and told her. There had been lots of shells about there, and the noise did not seem greater than that of some of those just close by.

The De Beers big gun kept pounding away in answer to all this, but was only one against eight or nine, and, being quite new, the men were not used to her, and could not do much. We heard a day or two after this that one of her shells killed three Boers. More power to her! I wish it had been three thousand.

In the afternoon I usually take Agnes out with me most of the time, so I told her I had to go round into several of the places where the shells were coming pretty thick, and suggested that she had better stay at home. She, however, is very plucky, and does not worry about the shells a bit, so she said she would come the same as usual, for if a shell hit me, it might as well hit her too. We went along all round and did the work, but several shells came within a hundred yards of us. Wherever we went they seemed to follow us round.

In Beaconsfield, the gun with which they are trying to hit Rhodes and the Sanatorium dropped a shell fairly near us, and we picked a big chunk of it up in the main road a few minutes after, still hot. This gun gives Beaconsfield, and the main road leading from Kimberley past the Sanatorium to Beaconsfield, a very warm time. Several shells have dropped into the main road—one just in front of a tram full of people, one into the Sanatorium grounds, one right over it and through the canteen used by the Volunteers guarding it—without hurting anyone. One went through an outhouse on Ruffel's grounds. (Mrs. R. and Katie are in Cape Town.) Several fell just outside the hospital, and one

The Sanatorium (peace)

dropped in the Catholic Orphanage grounds.

This gun kept at it at intervals all Wednesday night, and some of the others chimed in now and then. We went to bed as usual, for our special guns seemed quiet, and we slept till about 4 a.m. Then something woke me, and I heard two shells go over the house, or very close by, and burst somewhere quite near. Our house faces the gun that fires these shells, so we concluded that downstairs was better than upstairs, I took our mattresses down into the hall and put them on the floor by the hat-stand, where the wall is thickest, and was just going to turn in when the mayor came to fetch me to see his wife. I went along to his house, and found the shells dropping very close there, but fortunately the patient did not know they were so near, and so was not nervous. The mayor sent me home in his own cart.

At my door I found a policeman who wanted me to go and see a family who had been smashed up by a shell. I drove straight off to the house he mentioned, and found two poor little children badly hurt. They were not in their own house, but just across the street where they had been carried. One, aged six, had his shoulder shattered and the whole side of his head and face torn open, besides other wounds; the other, a year or two younger, had an arm and a leg both broken badly, and several wounds in the chest. I put them both into the cart and sent them straight off to the hospital, and was then told that the mother was in her own house, also badly hurt. I went across and found her lying on the floor with her leg wrapped up in a towel. An ambulance man was there, who said he had just fastened it up and that it was a beastly wound. I sent the mounted policeman for the ambulance and told the man to bring her along to the hospital when the ambulance arrived. Another child was just grazed with a splinter of the shell.

They were all (mother and six children) just ready to begin breakfast when the shell came and burst right in the middle of them. The father is a Volunteer, and was away at one of the camps. It is queer that he is said to be a prominent member of the Bond and has all along said the Boers were in the right. Whether he thinks so now, I don't know.

I went straight off to the hospital and tackled the worst-hurt child. The arm was hopelessly injured, and I had to take it off at the shoulder joint. The head injury was a jagged wound from above and behind the ear to the corner of the mouth, turning the ear down on to the neck, breaking the jaw in two places, and just ploughing up all the side of the face. There was also a big wound on the other arm, and a fair-sized one on the hip. The wonder and the pity was that the poor

THE SANATORIUM (WAR) SHOWING MAXIM – GUN AND MR. RHODES

little chap was not killed outright. I fixed him up as well as I could, expecting him to die under my hands all the time, but he lived about three hours.

Watkins turned up while I was busy; he took on the other child, and I turned to, as soon as I was free, and fixed up the mother. She had all the fleshy part of the calf ripped up right to the bone, and the wound went down to the heel. I was very doubtful whether I ought not to take the leg off there and then, but there seemed a possible chance of saving it, so I fixed it up as well as I could and awaited developments. She was a rather flabby individual who had only been confined three weeks, so the developments soon turned up. Forty-eight hours after, the leg was beginning to go gangrenous, and I took it off above the knee. Today, seventy-two hours after, she is better than she has been yet, but is not by any means out of the wood yet. And this is what the Boers call fair play!

Of the previous bombardment their commandant wrote to his chiefs that he directed his guns to the middle of the town to do as much damage as possible, and this is their aim again now. They must know that almost all the men are in the forts, and that very few people except women and children are left in the town, and yet they fire, not at the forts, but into the town. I have no doubt they will say they fired at the forts and their shells went too far, but we shall not believe that.

All that day the shelling went on until about 9.30 p.m., and since then we have had practically none. Twice that afternoon I very narrowly escaped a shell. At one house I called at, I was talking on the verandah for some time, and within twenty minutes of that a shell fell into the garden between the verandah and the road, not ten feet from where I had been; and again, I had just gone across to the Market Square at Beaconsfield and got to the corner, when a shell fell just where I had crossed not one minute before.

No one can imagine the relief it was when the shelling ceased. It is not altogether a question of fear, but the knowledge that wherever you are, a shell may drop on you at any moment, and that you have to do your work, all the same, does not much exhilarate you. I suppose if a doctor gets killed on duty, his patients will promptly say what a fool he was to come out, but if he stays at home, they say he is a cowardly cur for doing so. Any stick is good enough to whack a doctor with.

Today (Sunday) I don't think a shot has been fired on either side, but there are heaps of rumours as to what is in store for us tomorrow. More guns, bigger guns, and closer to us, is what most of the rumours amount to, but no one will know whether there is any truth in them till tomorrow. Nearly all the town has been busy building shellproof shelters, but we have decided not to do so. Our house is pretty solid, and unless they bring very big guns to bear upon us, we are only liable to be reached by the shells that come from the long side of the house, in the direction in which most of the windows face. If we keep in the bottom story and in the hall, I do not think we can be damaged. All the shells that have burst, did it in the first room they came to, and the pieces only went through into the second if the wall was very flimsy. Our walls are good and solid, so I think we should be pretty well all right in the hall, either where the bookcase is or at the other end by the hat-stand.

The shellproof places are ghastly little dog-holes—like the Black Hole of Calcutta in most cases. Some of the rich people have put up good ones, double layers of sand-bags built up on their verandahs to a decent height, and roofed either with sheet steel or old railway iron or thick deals with plenty of sandbags on the top of them; and in these there has been some attempt at ventilation; but the poorer people have dug holes in their yards or gardens and roofed them with anything that came handy, and then either just sandbags or the loose earth out of the hole was put on top. In these you can't stand up, and there is no ventilation at all, so I guess they would be about as deadly as the Boer shells; but lots of people seem to find comfort in being in them. One woman I know fled into hers early on the Wednesday morning, and never came out till late Friday afternoon; but she is the one who had a shell through her house in the first bombardment (and who gave us a piece of it), so she was likely to be timid.

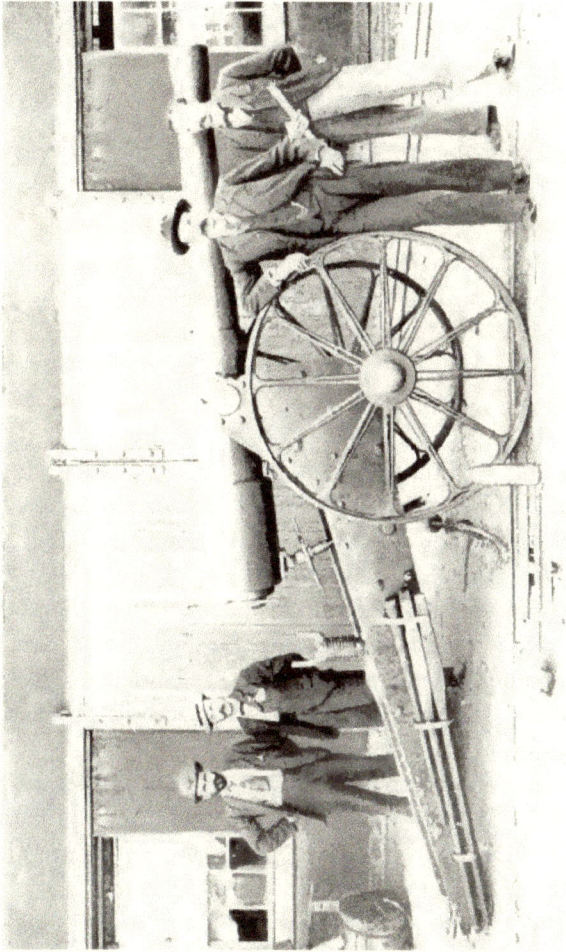

"Long Cecil"

CHAPTER 8

Our Big Gun,
and the Boers' Bigger One

Now, having finished about the bombardment whilst it was fresh in my mind, I must hark back and tell you about the De Beers gun. We had heard rumours that a big gun was being made for some time before the second bombardment, and we soon heard from the men at the De Beers machine shops that it was true. I did not go down to see it until it was nearly done; but I looked in a few days before it was completed, and took Agnes down next day, as she was interested in it. The gun has since been christened "Long Cecil," but many of us prefer other names for it; my favourite is "The De Beers Baby," but another good one is "St. Cecilia." It is a splendid piece of work, especially when you consider that many of the tools necessary to do the rifling and other complicated work had to be made in the shops, and that the men were not used to the work, and that even the material used was only, so to speak, makeshift.

The gun is about ten feet long, and is built upon the "Woolwich Infant" principle—slender near the muzzle, thicker in the middle, and very much thicker at the breech. The narrow part is about nine or ten inches through, and the thickest part at the breech about twenty or so. The shell it carries is 4.1 inches in diameter, and weighs twenty-eight and a half pounds, so if it drops on a Boer's head, he will probably know about it. Of course a proper gun-carriage and everything complete was made at the same time, and at last all was in order. There was great speculation as to what would happen the first time the gun was fired, but all the people principally concerned were confident he would be all right, and so he was.

They took him out of the shop on the morning of January 19th,

88

and pointed him at the midway pumping-station, half-way from here to Riverton, about six thousand five hundred yards from where he was fired, and let him go. To everybody's delight, he reached it quite easily. The Boers have had a big camp there all the time, as it was out of reach of our other guns, and there were good buildings and plenty of water there. After a few shells had been dropped pretty close, the Boers were seen to be buzzing about and departing like a hive of bees when a brick is thrown into it. A few days afterwards, our men caught a Dutch despatch-rider, and on him was a letter from a Boer to his home people, describing their consternation when the shells began to drop about them as they were at breakfast. They just got up and scooted, leaving their breakfasts behind.

The gun did very good shooting that day, but they took him back to the shop to make the powder-chamber larger, so that it would hold seven pounds of powder instead of five and a half, and so increase his range; but somehow this did not seem to improve his shooting, and though he has done good work during the bombardment, the men seem to think he is not so accurate as before.

On the same day that the gun was tried, I see in my diary that we had a new vegetable issued to us—the common or household mangel-wurzel. Horseflesh and wurzel do not sound luxurious, but they would be all right if there were only plenty of them. The wurzels are the Globe yellow sort, and are very good, not to be distinguished from beet except by the colour.

February 2nd.—Thank goodness, the expected heavy bombardment has not come off. Every day a few shells have dropped in, but only a very few—most days only three or four—so we have had quite a holiday. "Long Cecil" fired one shot early on Monday and no more, and later on we learned that he busted something with that shot and had to go back to the shop again. He was to have been all right again today, but has not been fired, so perhaps he is still out of gear.

All this time I have been wanting to send you some money, as I am afraid you will be hard up. I kept waiting and waiting, hoping that we should get communication, but early in January I thought I would wait no more. I went to the bank and got a draft in duplicate just in the usual way, and then I got the military people to let me send the duplicate drafts off by their despatch-riders, with a short letter, on two different nights, hoping that at least one of them would manage to get through. About a week after this, the banks made an arrangement by which the military would flash money to the column, and so on to

Cape Town, by the searchlight. So then I wished I had waited a little longer.

About a month afterwards, the military told me that neither of the despatch-riders had got through, and neither of them had returned, so they were either dead or prisoners. This was cheerful, for my drafts were probably in the hands of the Boers. I don't think it likely that anyone else but you could get the money, for the London bank has always had your draft come to them through the same channel all these years, so they would be suspicious if it came into their hands in any other way, especially at these times. They know your signature, too, and therefore there would be little risk, unless they really were criminally careless.

All the same, as we could get communication, I thought it wiser to stop that draft by cable from Cape Town, and to tell the Cape Town bank to post another draft to you. This was on January 26th, and next day I cabled to you that we were safe and well. I expected you would know in England that we were heavily bombarded on the 25th and 26th, so I thought that you had better know that we were all right after it all. I have sent off several wires to you, since the siege began, at intervals of three or four weeks, but have no means of knowing whether any of them got through or not.

February 4th.—Today we have had a new sort of food, donkey- instead of horse-flesh. The butcher who serves me always delights in trying to harrow up my feelings by telling me what the meat is, but I guess he will soon give up, for I always say: "All right, as long as it is meat, it is all the same to me." A few days ago my driver told me that a Chinaman had been offering Mackenzie's driver a good price for cats, which he wanted to eat—five shillings and sixpence for small ones and twelve-and-six for large ones. We have not come to that yet, but the Chinese are fond of cats at all times.

The bread ration in town has been cut down within the last few days. Previously it was fourteen ounces per head, now it is only ten and a half, so stores have to be husbanded a good deal. For the last few weeks we doctors, or rather the careful and conscientious ones of us, have been having an awful time with food permits. The regular rations issued consist of bread, horseflesh or beef, *mealie* meal, and crushed *mealies*, with vegetables about once in ten days, and tea or coffee and sugar. For the last few weeks nothing more of any description is al- lowed to be sold without a doctor's written order.

The doctors all have orders not to give permits except in cases where the people are sick, and then only in very moderate quantities. As I have told you before, every patient you have ever seen comes up and demands a permit for something, many of them being manifestly in robust health. The usual story is: "I won't eat horseflesh, and so I must have something else." My answer to these people has invariably been:

> Our orders are that we are not in any way to help people who refuse to eat horseflesh, therefore you can wait till you are hungry enough to eat it, or you can starve. You will get no permit from me.

The fat Jews, who have always lived on the best of everything, naturally do not like this, and so they go off to some other man they can bully, blarney, or bribe, and get whatever they choose to ask for, cursing me fluently all the time. They say their religion forbids them to eat horse, so as a rule they ask for bacon.

Some of the doctors are notorious for giving permits for anything to anybody. I am afraid I am notorious in the other way, having the reputation of giving "nothink to nobody," and consequently am not particularly beloved. However, I have done the square thing, and none of my sick people have had any reasonable request refused; but the loafers and guzzlers have had a bad time at my hands.

FACSIMILE OF MEDICAL COMFORT CERTIFICATE

None of this bother would have arisen if the Army doctor, who is really responsible for the proper issue of the medical comforts, had been a man of grit; but though a nice enough fellow, he has no backbone, and is too fond of red tape and sealing-wax. If he had gone into things a bit, he would easily have found out the offending men; and then, if he had been the right sort, he would have got the colonel to give him a free hand, and then would have gone to each offender, and talked like this: "Look here, my child, you are not playing the game. I give you fair warning that if you don't draw in your horns, I will refuse to recognise your signature on any permit, and don't you forget it."

That is the sort of yarn I would have reeled off to them, and I would have run the permit business satisfactorily inside a week if I had been responsible; but he is too mild, and the colonel is too busy to tackle the job in earnest.

At last, about a week ago, the Food Supply Committee struck over the business, and told the colonel that this permit system was being scandalously abused, as the comforts meant for the sick were being frittered away on perfectly healthy and strong people. The colonel appointed a committee to inquire into it, and both Mackenzie and I were members of it. I had on several occasions worried the colonel myself, so he knew I was interested in it.

We devised a stringent system of issuing permits and their supervision, which I hope will work much better, but the supervisor is hopeless; he seems absolutely to have no savvy whatever. For instance, one rule is that no patient shall draw more than one comfort, except in cases of urgent need, and these cases must have a written explanation of the urgency of their need on the back of their permit. The sensible way seems to me to be this: issue one of the things ordered at once, and go down to the patient's house and satisfy yourself that the others are really required before issuing them.

But Mr. Wronghead says issue all the things at once, and then go and see if they were really needed. As if either doctor or patient would care what happened, as long as the things were got. I did get a penal clause put into the rules, providing that any doctor not acting up to them should, at the discretion of the colonel, forfeit his right to sign permits, but I am afraid it won't be acted up to. These rules were just a month too late—in fact, on the first day they were in force the last tin of butter in the town was issued, and if it had been taken proper care of, and only issued to the sick, there would have been enough to last us through the siege.

After February 4th things jogged along quietly until the 7th. On that morning I was called to a confinement in one of the outlying parts of the town, rather near one part of the Boer lines. Whilst there, in addition to the usual intermittent shelling with both our and the Boer guns, I heard a much bigger gun begin. There was a big boom, then a tremendous whiz somewhere over or near the house I was in, and then, by-and-by, a good big boom when the shell burst. I was pleased at this, as I thought this was "Long Cecil" potting at the Boers at Carter's Farm, so I felt comfortable and happy. When I came out after it was all over, my driver, Daniel, looked pretty sick, and said: "The Boers have got a big gun at Kamfersdam, and are firing into the town with it." And so it was. He said the shells were falling near the Market Square, across which I wanted to go.

This looked cheerful, but I had to go up town, so we drove off. When we nearly got to the Square, we heard a shell bump into something fairly close to us, but we did not stay to inquire. Later on I found out that this shell had dropped into a house on the left side of the street, and a big piece of it flew across the road and killed a horse in a shoeing forge on the right side of the street, less than a hundred yards behind me. If I had been coming up about one minute later, that piece might quite easily have got me.

A piece of the same shell flew diagonally through an open window in the De Beers office at which a friend of mine was sitting. It went past him without touching him, struck an iron safe, bounced off that to the wall, and from there into the fireplace, where it stopped. The piece weighed eleven pounds, and my friend departed without waiting to put on his hat, and had three drinks one after the other before he began to feel better.

The gun kept on firing until midday, when it stopped to cool and let the Boers have dinner, but it started out again about three in the afternoon, and went at it hot and strong. About four I was at Ruffel's, calling for messages, and heard a big shell come over and burst not very far away, and then I came down to the house for tea. When I got near, I saw a lot of people rushing up the lane along the long side of the house, and I found that the shell had landed in our next-door neighbour's stable. There was a very sulphury smell in the air and a big cloud of dust, but our house seemed to be all right. I rushed indoors and called for Agnes, and she answered that she was all right, neither of the servants hurt, and the house untouched.

Agnes was upstairs putting on her hat to come out with me when she heard the shell whiz and explode, and saw the whole stable roof lift up. Fortunately the shell fell in soft ground and went in some way before it burst, so the pieces did not fly about, and beyond wrecking the building, no damage was done. Our house was filled with dust and smoke, and splinters of wood and roofing flew over into our garden. A few fair-sized stones came over too—one weighing about six pounds—and two whole sheets of galvanized iron: one fell on our beetroot bed, and the other cut the cord of the verandah blind and notched the verandah rail.

Our domestic took shelter under her bed, but was unearthed, unhurt, without difficulty. Agnes was ready to go out with me, so I took her, as she did not feel safe in the house. Up to this time she had stood the shelling splendidly, but this was coming a bit too close to be pleasant, and rather took the curl out of us both. Whilst we were on our rounds, we went into Ruffel's branch shop near the station, and a piece of shell had just dropped through the roof there, which they showed us. It was a solid piece of about eight pounds weight and an inch and a half thick, and showed us a little what these shells were like.

Later on (they were shelling all the time) we had to go into the De Beers workshops, and there we found one of the big shells which had not exploded. It had fallen out on the *veldt* at the back of the hospital. The people who picked it up took it to Rhodes, who gave them five pounds for it. He sent it down to the shops to have the powder taken out of it and to get it polished up. Down there they handled it very gingerly, for only a few weeks before we had had news from Mafeking of a blacksmith trying to open a similar shell when it exploded, blew off one of his legs and one of another man's, and killed a third man, so they had good reason to be careful, and accordingly let it soak in water for a few hours.

My driver had seen one of the men who picked this shell up, and told me he had said it was as big as the handbag that I carry instruments about in. Seeing that this came from a coloured man, of course I did not believe it, but it was under, rather than over, the truth. This infernal shell was eighteen and a half inches long and six inches in diameter at the base, and weighed eighty-seven pounds. We found later that the shells were not very accurately made, many of them being twenty inches long and weighing over one hundred pounds. As you can imagine, the sight of this shell did not encourage us, for we knew that a gun big enough to carry this shell could reach any part of

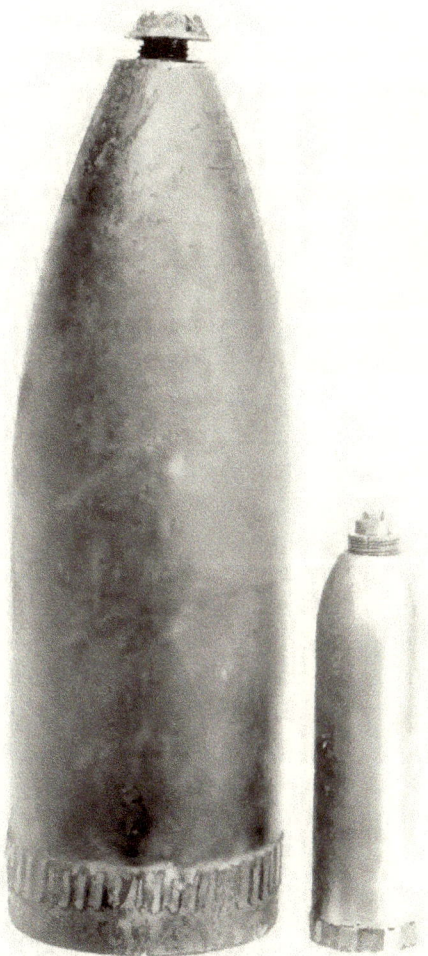

100LB. BOER SHELL   9LB. M. BOER SHELL

Kimberley or Beaconsfield, so that there was no possibility of getting out of its range, and we also saw that there was no building in Kimberley, except perhaps the strong-rooms at the banks, that would not be penetrated easily by it.

Fortunately the gun was fired from a place almost directly opposite the front door end of our house, so if we kept either in the little passage at the back of the dining-room or, better still, in the covered way between the house and the kitchen block, we should be fairly safe, for we had come to know from experience that a shell is usually exploded by the first wall it touches, but that it has sufficient impetus to carry it through that wall, and actually bursts in the first room it comes into. Coming from the direction they did, these shells would have to come through at least two pretty solid walls before they reached the other end of the house, so we felt fairly safe. The shelling went on until about dark, and then stopped, greatly to our relief. The damage done was not great; two men were hurt by splinters of wood, and a child was more seriously hurt and subsequently died, not exactly from the shell wound, but undoubtedly that helped.

Next morning we expected to be roused out quite early by the big gun, but to our great delight it did not start, so as the day crept on all sorts of rumours began to fly about, principally that "Long Cecil," who had been pounding away manfully at this Boer gun all the previous day, had smashed it up.

When lunch-time came and no big gun, we began to feel quite cheerful, but about four o'clock they began again, and for some time heaved a shell into us every two minutes, but they could not keep that up long, as of course the gun got hot and had to cool off. One of the early shells burst in the air, and a piece of it dropped through a roof near the bank and knocked a man's brains out, killing him on the spot. Another came through a photographer's opposite the club and burst on the pavement, and fragments of it flew on to the club verandah and out at the side, one of them rising high again and knocking the cross off the end of the Catholic Church at the side of the club.

A patient of mine got a chunk of this in his leg as he stood at the club. Just where the shell came through the photographer's wall, a big portrait of Rhodes hung, and the shell landed squarely in the middle of this and knocked it into smithereens. A little later on another shell dropped into a big shop next door to S.'s and set fire to it. The whole place burnt down, and S.'s place caught fire, but they managed to put it out.

When this happened, I had only just left S.'s private house, where I was seeing Mrs. S., who was ill. S. and I had been joking (we had to joke to keep up our spirits) about the shells, and he had asked me to give him some medicine to make his knees feel stronger when the gun went off, and the next minute his shop was nearly destroyed.

CHAPTER 9

The Rush for Shelter

Agnes still declared she did not want a shelter made on our premises, but I could see she was a good deal shaken by these infernal shells, so I went to Gardner Williams and asked him to let me have timber and iron from the De Beers stores, and a white overseer and some natives to build me a fort. He was very good, and consented at once. I felt sure Agnes would feel happier with a shelter, and we neither of us felt safe sleeping upstairs, when the gun was liable to fire at any moment, and the first shell might be the very one to drop on us, so we thought if we got a fort, we would sleep all night in it and not have to turn out first thing directly the gun went.

On this second day of the big gun a system of signalling was established which was a great help to us. The gun was firing ordinary powder and not cordite, and so made a big puff" of smoke. This could easily be seen from the conning tower and other prominent positions in the forts. Directly the lookout on the conning tower saw the puff, he waved a red flag, and a bugler standing by him blew the alarm. The gun was about three and a half miles from us, so there was an appreciable interval between the puff of smoke and the arrival of the shell. If the bugler got his little tune off smart, there was about fifteen seconds, and this gave you plenty of time to dodge under a wall or put up your umbrella (one man was actually seen to do this) or rush into your fort, but often the interval was much less.

At the Sanatorium there was a lookout station on the roof, from which the puff of smoke could be seen, and the look-out there banged on the dinner-gong for all he was worth directly he saw it. I thought Rhodes was having plenty of meals when I heard the gong going so often, until I found out that it was a shell signal.

At another place the look-out hammered one iron bar on another which was hung up by the end. This is a cheap sort of bell which is common in this country, and can be heard a long way. From many places people could see the red flag wave, though they did not hear the alarms. In front of the Town Hall a policeman was stationed in an auctioneer's pulpit to blow his whistle when he saw it. On the whole, we had heaps of music these days.

Next day (February 9th) was about the worst of all, as they pumped shells into us almost all day, only stopping for refreshments or to cool the gun. They began about 6 a.m. and went on till dark. About nine a shell went into a house near the station, killing a baby in its mother's arms and badly damaging the mother, ripping open one breast, blowing off part of a hand, and scratching and bruising her neck and chest, and fracturing her skull. At first she did well, but took a wrong turn about thirty hours after, and was dead in thirty-six.

Another shell went through a store close behind me when I was seeing patients at the office, and scattered pieces on the roof above my head; but I sat tight, and went on with the prescription I was writing. All the same, I was badly scared, for it is not nice to know that the last shells have fallen somewhere near you, and to hear the bugle go, and then go quietly on with what you are doing, with your ears pricked up for the boom of the gun and the whiz, wondering all the time whether this is the one that is going to get you or not. When you hear the shell bump into some other building and burst with a crash, you are happy at once, for you know you have got off once more.

We soon found that if the shells burst in a building, the pieces were stopped and could not fly; but if the shell burst in the air, or struck hard rock or road, they flew in a fearful manner, some of them going hundreds of yards, buzzing like a steam-saw all the time. These pieces were far more dangerous than the shell itself, and we did not like them a bit. A fair proportion of the shells did not explode; either because they were bad or because, as they were fired at a very short range for so big a gun, they struck on their sides and not on their points.

Some of them ricocheted off hard ground, and went half a mile before dropping again. The pieces sometimes weighed fifteen to twenty pounds, but more usually were from two to ten—and these were quite big enough.

By-and-by we found that there was a certain sort of method in the firing. They would point the gun at some particular object—the Town Hall and the conning tower being the favourite ones—and fire eight or ten shots till the gun was hot. Then they would point it somewhere else for eight or ten shots, and so on. As a matter of fact, their marksmanship was disgraceful; I don't think they once hit anything they aimed at, but they did a fair amount of damage all the same. Sometimes they departed from this rule and fired anyhow, no two shots in the same direction, and then things were not pleasant. Take it all round, it was not pleasant work going round to see your patients when the firing was on; but if they were firing in one quarter, you left those patients until they had slewed the gun round a bit to another quarter, and then went to see them.

I think the doctors' drivers had the worst job of all, for they had to sit in the carts and wait whilst we were in the houses. As a matter of fact, the houses were little, if any, safer than the open, but somehow you felt safer inside than out. Several drivers chucked up their jobs and hooked it, but mine stuck to his work like a brick and never flinched or hesitated wherever he had to go, though he admitted he was often badly scared. That was precisely my feeling. I was badly scared, but the work had to be done, and I felt that if a shell were destined to hit me, it would do so whether I were in or out, and whether in a shelter or not, and so, though I did not try to get hit, I went about my work as usual, and never missed a single ofiice hour or visiting a single patient on account of the shells. And I think all the doctors did the same. You bet my driver lost nothing by sticking to his post. When we were relieved, I gave him ten pounds, and our Zulu boy five pounds, for he had come and done his work just the same as usual.

It was) on this day (February 9th) that the De Beers people began to put up my splinter-proof shelter. It was put in the passage way between the dining-room and the storeroom, and the entrance to it was just outside the back door of the house proper. If you look at the plan of the house, you will see exactly where it was. The passage is nearly seven feet wide, and so there was plenty of room.

First of all strong steel plates five-eighths of an inch thick were put up against the wall of the dining-room, then a framework of huge mine props twelve inches thick was put up; the roof was made of similar timbers, and was seven feet high, and on the top of these another steel plate was laid.

The shells could not come from the kitchen side at all, so we just left that wall as it was. Then the two sides were built up with sacks filled with earth taken out of the garden and laid endways, so that a shell or splinter would have to come through quite two feet of earth before getting at us. We were late beginning our fort, so nearly all the

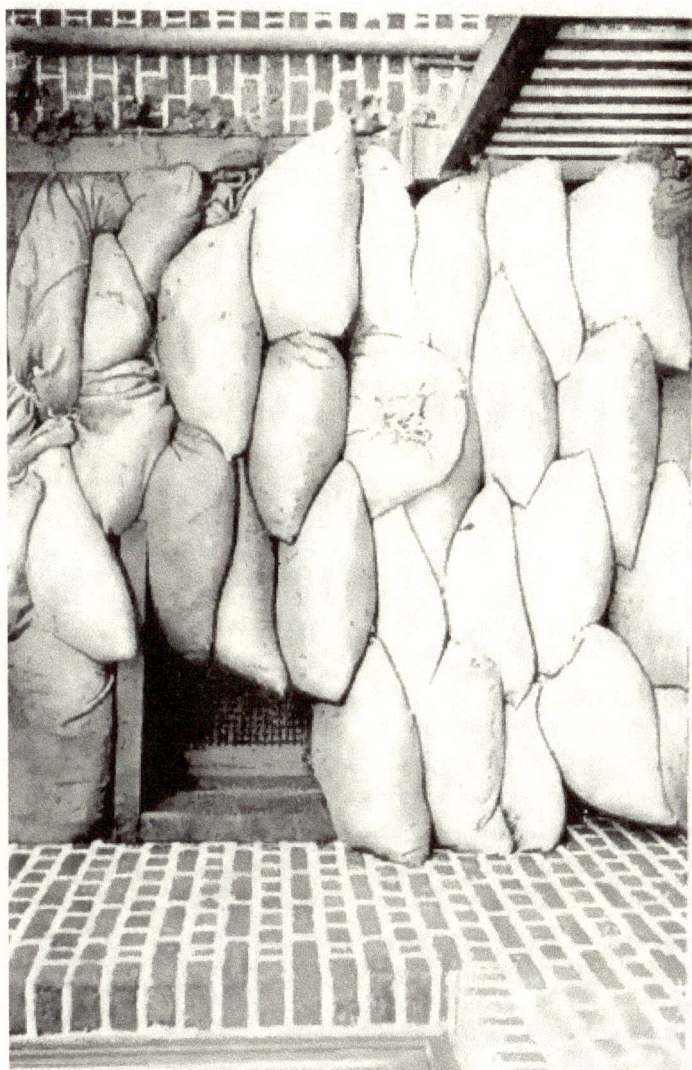

OUR SHELTER – WEST SIDE

sacks were gone; but I went round to several of the bakers and fos-
sicked out a good lot. It took a lot of earth to fill the sacks, and this had
to be dug out of the garden. I had a nice patch of barley growing for
my horses, but this all went into the sacks, together with lots of bulbs
and other garden-stuff. The bulbs will not be hurt, but the rest of the
truck will be beyond resurrection.

On the first day the fort did not make much progress, as the boys
were sawing the timbers the right length and getting the materials
together. I think they liked working here, for we gave them lime juice
to drink, as it was very hot, and they said they were very hungry, so
we gave them some big chunks of very coarse brown bread, which
they seemed to appreciate. Everybody was on short commons at this
time, so I expect the compound boys were getting very little except
mealie-meal porridge, and none too much of that.

By the way, I ought to have told you that at about this time I sold
one of my horses to be killed and eaten. He was one of the original
horses I bought when I took over the practice, and had done heaps of
good work for me. Before the war, as he was getting old, I turned him
out to grass on a farm, meaning to let him end his days in peace there,
getting him in for a few weeks now and then to relieve a sick or lame
horse. When the war broke out, I had to get him in, or let the Dutch
steal him. For a time I kept three horses, but now forage got so scarce
that I had to get along with two. I would never have sold him to be
worked and hammered about in a Scotch cart, but now it was a case of
either turning him out to die of starvation on the *veldt* or selling him
to be eaten. So I sent the old chap to the butcher, and he went to feed
the Lancashires. He fetched thirteen pounds,

I must tell you some more about the shelling on this same day
(February 9th). It went on till dark. One shell went through Watkins's
back fence, into a shed where carriages were stored, and smashed a
victoria into little bits, but did not explode, fortunately for Watkins.
Another (and this is about the most wonderful escape of the siege) fell
into a room where a lady was in bed, just missed her hip, broke the
side of the bedstead into bits, and harmlessly buried itself in the foun-
dation under the floor. Had it exploded, she would have been blown
into little bits, but it did not.

The last shell that night was the biggest tragedy of the siege. it went
into the Grand Hotel at the corner of the Market Square, and killed
George Labram, the chief engineer to the De Beers Company. He, of
all the people in Kimberley, had probably done more to frustrate the

plans of the Boers and make things unpleasant for them than anybody else. He fixed up the new water supply when our proper supply was cut off; he made the shells for our guns to use; and it was he who manufactured "Long Cecil," having to make many of the necessary tools for the rifling from his own ideas; and in many minor ways he had helped the military to worry the Boers.

He was an American, and just as smart as they make them, even in America, and was a first-rate fellow into the bargain. He had had several narrow shaves with the shells, but this day it seemed as if he were doomed. Coming away from the machine shops at half-past five a shell very nearly got him, and then he came to the hotel for dinner. His room was on the top floor, and the hotel was directly in the big gun's line of fire when it was aimed at the Town Hall, so it was not a safe place.

Labram stayed downstairs in the hotel till the firing seemed to have ceased, and then he went up to wash before dinner, and a final shell came along and killed him. He was shockingly mauled, half his head being caved in, also his chest and abdomen, and both his thighs were so smashed up that they just hung on by a few shreds. The only consolation was that death must have been instantaneous, and he can have felt no pain. One of the hotel servants was in the room at the same time, and he was not touched.

The poor chap's wife was away in America, so the De Beers Company arranged to have the body embalmed as well as they could, and have it soldered up in an air-tight coffin, so that he could be taken home and buried later on. This accident, as you may well imagine, cast a heavy gloom over us, for everybody knew and liked the man, and none of us could feel that it was not possibly his own turn next.

All this day, besides the work on private shelters, big public shelters were being made wherever there were convenient places. These were made by the De Beers Company's boys and the natives who were working on the roads for the Relief Committee, about which I will tell you later on. Most of the shelters were made in the sides of the *débris* heaps, which are almost all over the town. A deep trench was cut in the sloping side of the heaps, and then this was lined and roofed with timber and galvanized iron, and a thick layer of earth was thrown on to the top and hanked up against the front face of the shelter. Several of these shelters were many yards long and had several openings, so that people could get in and out easily.

In Beaconsfield, on one side of the main road, there was a big heap with an almost perpendicular face, and here they just drove tunnels straight into the heap. It looked very funny from the road to see these catacombs. The big bridge which carried the road over the railway near the station was made into a shelter by leaning timbers against the sides of it, putting steel plates next them, and then banking up with sandbags and loose earth. Many people who lived near the station took refuge under trenches in the big station building, and in the engine-sheds, in the ashpits, and under the engines, of which we had a dozen or more in Kimberley.

Speaking of the railway reminds me that a shell struck one of the rails near the station and knocked out a piece of rail twenty-two inches long, and deposited it upon the roof of an hotel over a hundred yards away.

All through the bombardment the people who lived near any of the culverts which carry the rain-water off used to shelter there when shelling was going on, and many of those who lived near *débris* heaps made their own private excavations there. All round the public gardens a wide drain, quite ten feet deep, runs, and many of the good-class people made shelters there by getting old railway rails or tram rails, and roofing a part of the drain in with these, piling loose earth on the top.

On the next day (Saturday, February 10th) we were all very depressed on account of Labram's death, and we expected heavy shelling again, but we had comparatively few shells that day. A few came in between 6 a.m. and 9 a.m., and then no more till about 4.30 p.m., but we had a few of the smaller shells from guns in other parts. These, however, we quite disregarded; after the big gun we cared for none of the smaller ones. They were to be treated as if the Boers were spitting at us.

Of course there were all sorts of reasons given why the big gun rested so long—it had burst, or they were short of ammunition, etc. The real reason was that some of our men had got into a position about seventeen hundred yards from the big gun, and made it lively for the men working it whenever they brought it out to fire.

We had at first thought that it was what is called a disappearing gun, which is worked from a deep pit, only being raised to be fired, but it was nothing of the sort; its carriage moved sideways, so it was hauled behind a strong fortification to be loaded and then pushed out to be sighted and fired, and directly it appeared from behind its shelter, our riflemen and big "Cecil" let rip at it and the men working it. They

DUGOUTS – SHELTERS FROM THE BOERS' 100 POUNDER

made it so warm for them that they did very little all day. Later on we heard that the two principal men on the gun were Frenchmen, and that one of our bullets curled one of them up, going clean through his head. This dodge of ours was kept up until we were relieved, and five or six of the men at the gun are said to have been killed altogether. Anyhow, it damped their ardour a good deal, and prevented them firing as much as they otherwise would have done.

I was fairly busy all the day, as I did an operation for a bad case and had a lot of other work besides. In several places I found my patients who were too ill to be up, lying on mattresses in their shelters, and ghastly little dog-kennels lots of them were. The entrances were of course very low and narrow, to prevent splinters of shell flying in, and I had to back down into them, just as I used to have to do into the North Sea fishing-smack cabins. The atmosphere of them reminded me of the smacks too, as they were fearfully hot, and in most of them there was not the least attempt at ventilation, though a few had pieces of iron piping stuck through the roof. During the day our own shelter advanced rapidly; the roof was all completed and the most exposed side built up to within about two feet of the roof, and the other side nearly finished too.

About half-past four the gun started again, and went along till about half-past six, but very little damage was done. One small piece came through the club verandah roof, and another slightly wounded one of the Lancashires. When the gun stopped, we congratulated ourselves that we had got off easily, but we were a bit too previous, Labram's funeral had been arranged for 8 p.m., for it was sure to be a very large one, and the Boers would be able to see it, and fire at the people following, by daylight, so it was decided to have it by night. Directly the procession left the hospital gates (it is said by people who were looking out) a rocket was sent up somewhere not far off the hospital, and the big gun started immediately, and put in four or five shells very close indeed to the funeral. Some infernal traitor had, no doubt, told the Boers all about the funeral arrangements, and sent up the rocket to let them know when it started. This sort of thing we had got quite used to, for our half-hearted special court (called "martial" because there are no soldiers in it) never convicted any traitor unless absolutely compelled.

When the funeral was over, we expected the shells to stop. I had to see a patient at the hospital, and two more in the main road between my house and there. At nine I started out, and when about a hundred yards or so away, I saw a big flash of light. As it was a dark, cloudy night, I thought this was lightning. Then I heard the bugle, but did not take much notice of it, as the bugle in the camp close by always goes at nine; but a minute after I heard the boom of the gun, and then the shell came along mighty near—so near that I cowered down under a galvanized iron fence, not that that would be any protection, but anyhow it *felt* safer. Some pieces of shell, or stones thrown up by the shell, rattled on the roofs round me. I picked myself up and moved on a little to the first patient I wanted to see. A few shells went whilst I was in the house, and when I came out, the patient's husband walked down his garden with me to the gate. Half-way down the garden, rip came a shell very close, and we both dropped flat and pulled in our heads and lay close like tortoises. The pieces dropped all round us, but we were not touched.

We picked ourselves up and felt over our bodies, just to see that no arms or legs or heads had dropped off, and then I moved on to the next patient—the one on whom I had operated that afternoon. She was well under morphia, but the shells were dropping all round her house and had frightened her a good deal. Whilst I was seeing her, one burst close by, and the pieces rattled on the roof of the room she was in. When I left her, I stayed on the front verandah for a couple of minutes talking to her husband, and whilst there, "bang" came a shell into a house exactly opposite where I was, but on the other side of the road. Then I went on to the hospital.

Shelling is bad enough in the daytime, but it is heaps worse at night. In the day you can see where the shell lands, and if it is not too close, you feel all right, but at night, first you hear the bugle and you try to sit tight and pretend you did not hear it, then comes the "boom" and "whiz," and you have to pretend harder than ever. Even when the shell bursts and you know that one, at any rate, has not got you, you don't feel happy for another minute or so, for the splinters fly so, that there is plenty of time for you to congratulate yourself on escaping the shell and then get your head caved in by a splinter.

After I got to the hospital the shells did not seem to be quite so close. I sat on the verandah with the doctors, and yarned to them and listened to the music for quite an hour and a half. I wanted to get off home, as I knew Agnes would imagine that I had butted up against a shell, but all the same, good as home seemed to be, where I was was plenty good enough, as the shells were falling then. One landed fairly near the hospital, and a good-sized piece of it came through the roof of one of the outlying wards, struck a lamp that was burning, and smashed it, carrying away a thick iron bar that supported it, but none of the patients were hit and nothing was set on fire.

After half-past ten the firing slackened a little, and on timing the shells there seemed to be about eight minutes between them, so I thought I would have time to get home between two, but then they began again quickly, so I did not start. We expected they would stop at midnight, as the Boers are consistent in that one respect—they don't fight on Sunday. Later on, about a quarter-past eleven, I determined to come home after the next shell, and risk getting hit; so when it had come, I started, but was stopped at the lodge-gate by a man who wanted to take me off to a case. I sent him off to get a cab, as it was a good long way off, and started for home myself, and as luck would have it, there were no more shells. I believe the Dutch were going by Transvaal time, and so twenty-five minutes past eleven with us is twelve with them.

Agnes had been sitting in our fort, which was nearly finished, and fancying that every shell had struck me. Many of those I had heard had gone very near to the house, and one only just missed it, bursting about one hundred and fifty yards farther on. After the case was over, I went off to bed quite calmly, as I felt sure that we should have a rest all the next day, and so it proved. All the same, I turned out as soon as it was light (at about 5 a.m.), to finish my fort. I was not at all sure that the boys would turn up to work on Sunday, so, as there was not much to do, I thought I would get it finished myself.

I had some sacks left, and I began to fill these, but you don't make much progress shovelling with one hand and holding the sack open with the other. By-and-by Agnes looked over the top verandah to see what I was after, and, seeing how awkward it was, she came down and held the sacks open whilst I shovelled. We had about eighteen sacks, and just as they were all full the miner and the natives turned up.

There was not very much to do, really, except fill up about two feet of one side of the fort, but as the boys had turned up, I got them to alter the other side, where the entrance was. They had made a square entrance just like a doorway, and very much too large, so that fragments of shells could come in quite easily, if they came in the right direction. I made them build a sort of projecting spur in front of the opening, so that no piece could possibly fly in unless it had first come through the house. I made them narrow the doorway very much, leaving only just room to squeeze in, and then you did not want to eat too much dinner or you would stick fast. This, however, did not matter so much on siege fare, as big dinners were not easy to get.

When this work was done, I still wanted a lot of sacks to make the place secure, so I went down to Dr. Stoney's brother and got some from him. He had promised me a few, but I found he could let me have a lot—far more than the boy I took with me could carry. He lent me his Scotch cart and two horses, and we tumbled the sacks in. Of course I rode home on the top of the pile, much to the amusement of Dr. Stoney and his brother, who stood on their verandah and jeered at me. Dr. Stoney's only regret was that his camera was out of gear, as he said "the sight of Kimberley's boss doctor sitting on a pile of sacks in a Scotch cart, and clad in dirty flannels and big Boer hat, and with a little Hottentot as driver and a raw *Kaffir* in a red shirt as footman, was too good to be lost." One of my best patients cut me dead on the way up, as he did not recognise me, though nobody worried much about clothes these times.

With the fresh lot of sacks, the boys finished up the fort in style. I had been in too many stuffy forts that week to neglect ventilation in my own, so I built in a strong iron grating opposite to the entrance, in a place where it was practically impossible for any bit of shell to come, and it answered splendidly. There was a nice through current of air all the time. When the miner took his boys away, he said: "I don't know anything about shells, but if the whole house falls on that fort, it won't hurt."

That was my view too. If the big gun kept in the same place, we were absolutely safe; but if they started others in different quarters, we might not feel so happy. The fort was seven feet square and seven high, so my six feet three had heaps of room in every direction. Agnes pinned sheets and big bath-towels all round the walls inside, and brought our bedding and mattresses down into it, with a looking-glass, a clock, some books, a box of sweets, and all sorts of other gear, and we had provisions close by if things were really bad, so when we had pinned a photo of Kitchener on the wall with a big diamond brooch, we felt as jolly as could be expected. We slept in the fort every night after that, for the Boers often started their gun at daylight, and if we were upstairs, we had to keep our ears pricked to hear the first shot and then bolt for the fort, whilst if we were in the fort, we slumbered calmly, feeling that if a shell did happen to get us there, destiny must be very decidedly against us, as it would have to work so hard to find us.

The photo of the fort shows its construction on the west side and

THE CONVENT SHELTER

the ventilating grating.

Our servants were told that they could come into it any time they heard the bugle. Lizzie came in for a few times, when she was handy, but as a rule did not bother, and was really very plucky. John, our Zulu, preferred to get behind the big water tank. I don't think that would have saved him, but he was happy there, so that was all right. He was very funny one day. We heard Lizzie lecturing him about something, and he retorted: "Don't make such a noise; I can't hear the gun go off." The boom of that gun would have extinguished a megaphone, so that was a great tribute to Lizzie's vocal powers.

I shall not forget this Sunday in a hurry. It *was* a day. First of all, everybody was so delighted that it was Sunday, as that meant rest from the shells. Kimberley is not exactly composed of Sunday-school superintendents, and as a rule is rather bored by Sundays, but not this one. Then, again, everywhere you went, forts were being built, and the clang of sheet steel, railway rails, old iron railway sleepers, etc., etc., was heard all over the place. The streets were full of carts and handcarts and wheelbarrows, and even natives carrying materials for forts. Many people could not get boys, as the demand was so great for labour, and so they had to do the work themselves.

Several of the merchants had large stocks of the coarse Boer salt, which is got by crystallisation from the salt pans, and they made forts of this. It is packed in large sacks, and answered splendidly. In the first bombardment, I had seen at a baker's a fort made entirely of sacks of flour. It was very good, but all the same, I was just as pleased I did not deal with that particular baker. But the gem of the collection in the way of forts was one I saw in the Malay camp. It belonged to a *coolie*, and he had a large dog in a kennel. He evicted the dog and banked up the kennel with old zinc baths and paraffin tins filled with earth, and I have no doubt was a little king in that yard, as nobody else had a fort at all there.

Towards afternoon the vague rumours of heavy bombardment beginning directly after midnight began to take shape, but the shape was different in each house. Anyhow, everybody was sure that Monday was going to be a bad day, and whether there were to be two new big guns or twenty was immaterial. Early in the afternoon notices signed by Mr. Rhodes were posted up in many places, and sent around the town on a cart, to the effect that women and children were advised to take shelter in the two big mines. It was promised that arrangements would be made to lower them down, and make them as comfortable

The Public Works' Department shelter

as possible. This being signed by Mr. Rhodes was looked upon as a confirmation of the rumours, as many people at once concluded that Mr. Rhodes had had private information as to what was going to happen on the morrow, and a regular panic ensued.

SUNDAY. I.RECOMMEND.WOMEN AND.CHILDREN.WHO.DESIRE COMPLETE.SHELTER.TO.PROCEED TO.KIMBERLEY.AND.DE-BEERS SHAFTS. THEY.WILL.BE.LOWERED AT.ONCE.IN.THE.MINES.FROM 8.O'CLOCK.THROUGHOUT.THE.NIGHT. LAMPS.&.GUIDES.WILL.BE PROVIDED. C.J.RHODES

CHAPTER 10

A New Use for Diamond-Mines

Later in the afternoon the streets were again filled, but this time with people hurrying to the mines with their children, some carrying their babies, others carrying blankets or bedding, others food, but all loaded up with something. Cabs could not be got, all the horses being turned out to earn their own living, as there was no forage left except for the military horses, and so everyone had to walk. As I went round seeing my patients, I was asked by them all what I advised them to do. I know the mines pretty well down below, and though the places the people would go to were cool and lofty, my advice always was: "If you have a fairly strong fort of your own, don't go down below." This seemed sense to me, for there must be intervals between the firing during which you could get food and a bath and so on, and the prospect of being shut up in the same compartment with about a hundred children did not seem sufficiently alluring to compensate for the extra danger incurred by staying above ground.

I believe Mr. Rhodes's original intention was to offer shelter in the mines to those who had no place of shelter to go to, or who had insufficient protection of their own. Many of the poor people had no means of making shelters for themselves, and could neither afford the material nor the labour necessary to make one, and it was to these that the mines were offered. The notice, however, did not state so, and many better-class people went down. The mine-heads were crowded with people, and though they began to lower them down at about 5.30 p.m., it was long after midnight before they were all in the mines. More than a thousand went down Kimberley Mine, and about fifteen hundred were taken down in De Beers' Mine, yet neither in letting them down nor hauling them up again nor during their four days' stay down below was there a single accident to any one of them.

115

BARKLY ROAD BARRIER WITH MR. RHODES'S NOTICE IN POSITION

All this time provisions, or, rather, luxuries, had been getting dearer. We had a fowl for dinner, price fifteen shillings, and we bought some eggs for twenty-two shillings a dozen. Vegetables were very scarce, and often unprocurable. We used to make salad of a weed that grew in our garden. We had planted several beds of things that did not come up, or died from want of water, but this weed came up instead, and very handy we found it.

Shelling began at about seven on Monday, February 22nd, but in a half-hearted sort of a way, and not much damage was done—in fact, the whole day's performance was a pleasant surprise, as we had expected a very lively time. Our old friend was still the only big gun at work. The streets were almost deserted, for in addition to the people who had gone down the mine, many others had gone to Beaconsfield for safety. Beaconsfield lies at the foot of a hill, and Kimberley on the top of it, so Beaconsfield is not visible from where the big gun fires, and as there is an open space nearly half a mile wide between the two places, I expect the Boers thought they were as likely to hit the space as the houses, and did not care to waste shells.

The patient I operated on on Saturday moved down yesterday, also the man whose leg was hit by a piece of shell a few days ago. The gun could reach Beaconsfield with the greatest ease, and soon after this last man moved, a big shell landed fairly close to his house there, but that was the only one that got so far. The shells which flew such a distance were curious to listen to. When this one went off, I was at a house about as near to the gun as I could go. We heard the shell go over, and then its noise became more and more indistinct, until, when far away, the usual whiz seemed to be quite lost, and the noise reminded me of an empty cart galloping down a country lane far away on a still night. Then it plunged into something and burst.

One of the shells fired a block of four houses in Kenilworth today, but I do not think they were burnt out. Another struck the street about twenty yards from a house where one of my private nurses was nursing a patient. It did not burst, but bounced off again through an iron fence, making a big clatter, and disappeared nobody knows where. The nurse was splendidly plucky, and so was the patient. The house in which they were was near the foot of the conning tower, and therefore was liable to be hit at any time, but neither nurse nor patient wanted any shelter. The patient lay calmly in bed and said she did not expect she would get hurt, and the nurse never flinched, but looked after her like a brick. The nurse took me to look over the back fence at a sight I don't expect to see again. This was a lot of *Kaffir* women building themselves a shelter with heavy mine timbers. Everybody was busy, and no one could be spared to fix them up, so they were told that there was the timber and they could build for themselves, and they did.

Today a shell went through a nice, new two-storied house not so far from the Sanatorium. It was built soon after mine, and by the same architect (Jarvis). He always professed to believe that the Boers were in the right, but how he will feel when he hears that they have wrecked one of his very special houses, I don't know. There were twelve people scattered about the house, and not one of them was touched, but pretty well all the upper story was wrecked, and will have to be rebuilt, A suit of clothes hanging up was riddled to such an extent that three more tears would have caused them to fall into little bits. They were a sight: no self-respecting scarecrow would be seen dead beside them.

Another shell burst in the hospital grounds, about twenty yards from the side of a ward full of patients, and later on a shell dropped into an aloe thicket in the hospital grounds, but did not burst. These aloes are very thick and tough, so they stopped the shell without leaving a mark on it. It is the nicest specimen I have seen, and will, I have no doubt, be mounted and put in the entrance hall at the hospital as a trophy if we ever do come out of our troubles right side up. The hospital porter fished it out of the aloes and commenced to experiment upon it with a stick, giving it a good old stir up and smoking all the time. Dr. Russell admired his zeal, but thought him lacking in discretion, and made him put it in a tub of water before he proceeded with his experiments.

By the way, a friend told me a lovely yarn about one of these big shells today. Wherever a shell falls, whether it bursts or not, there is a rush for it, as both shell and pieces are marketable, if you don't wish to stick to them yourself. My friend was out with the cattle guard, and a big shell fell close to two natives who were with him, and did not explode. It was rather too hot to carry off, so they fought vigorously for possession, and the victor then sat down on it, to take care of it till it had cooled down enough for him to take it away.

I heard of another little joke today which amused me mightily. A certain man built a large and fine A1 copper-bottomed fort. A neighbour came to inspect it, and found great fault with it—in fact, condemned it altogether, and strongly advised the proud owner to take his family down the mine for safety. This he promptly did. Then the

THE RIGHT HON. CECIL RHODES

neighbour, having a very rotten fort of his own, took possession of the good one with equal promptness, and all was peace. (N.B.—The band played later.)

Today we had no newspaper, but a little slip came out, saying that for reasons that would be explained afterwards, the paper had shut down for a time. We none of us required an explanation, for we all expected this to happen today. For some time there had been friction between the paper and the military censor, as he refused to let anything but the vaguest accounts of the siege and our general condition be heliographed through. When the big gun started, several correspondents tried to wire through about it, as it seemed to us that it was time for our relief column to get up and hustle a bit. But that was not the censor's idea. He flatly refused to let any information of the use of a bigger gun go through at all. Whether he actually got it out or not, I do not know; if he didn't, this was on the tip of his tongue: "It might interfere with the military situation."

Oh, Lord! that "military situation." It was the answer to every conundrum you liked to ask all through the siege. After this the paper got mad, and on Saturday morning dodged the censor and came out with a very strong leader on the foolishness of such censorship, and just walked into the military people all round. So we were not surprised to get no paper today, and we were not particularly disappointed, for there was no news in the paper at all, and we had got a little tired of stories of the Battle of Waterloo, and other ancient history with which the dearth of news had been helped out. Even the Mother Seigel man had ceased to trot out new pitfalls in the way of advertisements. I do not think the paper was suppressed, but as the military possessed all the channels of information, I guess they shut them all up. The result was the same: no paper.

February 13th.—We had rather a rest from the shells today. Only about twenty came in altogether, but they did a fair amount of damage, all the same, and got on people's nerves a good deal. Many of my patients stayed in their shelters all the time, and as it was a hot day and many of the shelters were very small and stuffy, they suffered accordingly. One shell struck the Presbyterian Church. The English Church had been hit in the first bombardment, but the Dutch Church escaped altogether. It was curious to notice that many people among the Dutch took shelter in their church when the shelling was on; either they had greater faith than the other religions, or, what is far more likely, they had had word from their friends on the outside that the church would not be shelled. We had heaps of traitors in the place, who went to and fro much as they pleased; and though I don't think the gunners could see the Dutch Church, I have no doubt they had accurate plans of the town, and could locate all the big buildings.

Two shells went into Nazareth House (the Catholic orphanage), or, rather, one dropped just at the back door, and the other burst overhead, and a big bit of it went through the roof into the sisters' sitting-room. This last was a shrapnel, and was the first of the big gun shrapnels I had seen. They are not quite the same as the smaller ones we had got to know before. They have a big, solid base weighing fourteen pounds. On to this a thin steel sheet is fastened to make the receptacle for the bullets. The bullets are about the size of ordinary marbles, and are not loose, but lie in holes in cast-iron discs, like marbles on a solitaire board.

These discs are not solid, but are divided up into lots of small pieces by deep notches, which are so arranged that when the shell bursts, the pieces will come apart easily, and fly about like the bullets; but each piece has about a dozen jagged corners and would make a ghastly wound. The discs are threaded on a wide copper tube, which conducts the flame from the fuse at the point of the shell to the charge near its base, which rips the shell open when it bursts. The steel case takes up all sorts of outlandish shapes, as it does not fly to pieces, but just gets bent and twisted up, making very queer noises as it flies through the air. I heard one whistle just like a hooter. This particular Nazareth one looked more like the breastplate of an ancient suit of armour or a dilapidated soup tureen than anything else.

I forgot to say that on Sunday Rhodes somehow got a message from Lord Roberts to the effect that the column was going to move to our relief at once, and every day we heard rumours of heavy firing on both sides of Spytfontein, but nothing has come of it so far.

February 14th.—Today has been a great day. We do at last seem to have beaten the wily Boer on his own ground. Shelling began about as early as usual, but they treated us to some small shells from a gun in their old position near the *lazaretto*, and one of these killed a man working in a bakery quite early in the morning. The big gun was evidently trying for the Army Office just behind us, for several of its shells came rather close to us when we were at breakfast. I hate to be disturbed at my meals, either by patients or shells, so I sat tight and proceeded. I had got well used to shells by this time, and though I had the instinct to take cover whenever I heard a shell very well developed, I managed to resist it. We all had found that the only thing to do was to take a good grip of yourself and sit fast. If you once gave way and let yourself go, it was all up, and you had to strike out for the shelter every time the bugle went. I was seeing a patient in my office at the chemist's a few days before, when a shell dumped itself into a store next door but one. I felt that I was urgently needed elsewhere, but still I went on talking and fixed up the patient before I went downstairs, though the pieces pattered on the window and roof.

However, to return to breakfast. Just as we were finishing, a shell came very close, and when we rushed out to see where it was, we found it had fallen and burst in the street just at the end of our yard. This was a shrapnel too, but one of those that only explode when they strike, and so much less dangerous than the time-fuse ones, which burst overhead and rain bullets down on you. I think the Boers had used all their stock of solid shells, for I saw several shells during the day, and they were all this kind of shrapnel.

Yesterday the fourteen-pound base of one of these went through the water tank which stands at the corner of the nurses' home at the hospital. That was the third in the hospital grounds, and today several flew right over the hospital. One poor chap, a patient of mine, was so terrified by them that he insisted on going out, though his own place is much nearer the gun. He is very ill, and will not be able to get much attention at home, so I am afraid he will die.

I hardly think even the Boers intend to hit the hospital. These were merely bad shots at the Sanatorium, where Mr. Rhodes is staying. The shot which killed Labram was a bad shot at the Town Hall, and the one which killed the woman and child I spoke of earlier on was a bad shot at the conning tower. They have never yet hit a thing they aimed at, but they have done some damage, all the same.

The most wonderful shell of all was one which fell today at Dr. Fuller's gate. It just ran its nose under the kerbstones at the edge of the pavement and burst there. Two big stones were flung aside, but the biggest one, a solid blue whinstone block about twenty inches long by six inches wide and ten inches deep, was thrown right up on to the roof of the house, and from there slid gently down and lodged on the roof of the second-storey verandah, quite twenty feet above the street. There it lies now. I hope some photographer will take a snap at it there, or you will think someone else lies, as well as the stone.

So much for the Boers' day's work; now for ours. Early in the morning some natives came from Alexandersfontein to Beaconsfield, and said that the Boers there had all cleared out to help another commando, which was in difficulties, or wanted to do something funny, and was not strong enough to do it single-handed, or something of that sort. The Beaconsfield Town Guard was a bit suspicious of a trap, but sent out spies to investigate, for Alexandersfontein was an important position for the Boers, as there was plenty of water there, and it was only about four miles from Beaconsfield.

The spies found the natives' story to be quite true, and some of the Town Guard, with help from the Lancashires, Light Horse, and Kimberley Rifles, went out and took possession. There were a few Boers there, but very few. Several were killed, and more wounded, amongst them a Dutch girl who was rather badly hurt in the left arm. Four Boers were taken prisoners. The girl was brought into the hospital as soon as possible, and attended to. It is a regular Dutch performance to take women and children to the front. They have women with all the commandoes around us. I expect they imagine they are going to have a gay time looting the Kimberley shops, but that has yet to come.

After our men had taken possession of Alexandersfontein, they lay low to wait for developments. Before long, four waggon-loads of provisions and stores for the Boers came along, and came right into our men's hands before the drivers realised that the scene had changed. There was any amount of stuff there besides these four waggon-loads, making about twelve loads altogether, so our men had a fine haul. There was butter, vegetables, grain, mutton, pigs, poultry, and all sorts of things that we had not seen for weeks. Some of the loot was sent up to Kimberley at once.

I met the procession as I was coming in to lunch. It was first-rate, and the people turned out delighted, hoping that this was the beginning of better things. First came about twenty horses, then about the same number of cattle, and then a big waggon with a water tank on it, and drawn by sixteen lovely bullocks, so fat that our mouths watered just from looking at them. On the front of the waggon stood a man I know in a statuesque attitude, with his rifle grounded, and an "I-did-it-though-you-wouldn't-think-it-of-me" expression on his face. Oh, it was great!—but the effect was rather spoiled by an excited *Kaffir* who was standing up on the waggon tilt just behind him, waving a riding-boot in each hand and shouting "Look, at Cronje's boots" in Dutch.

Our people sent out strong reinforcements to Alexandersfontein, for they knew that the Dutch would return presently and would han-

WESSELTON CONNING-TOWER

ker after those provisions, and as the place was on the flat, within easy artillery range of *kopjes* on three sides, they expected a pretty warm time—and they got it. Along in the afternoon the Boers returned, and did not take to the new order of things at all kindly, but commenced to make things hum, both with rifles and artillery. Fortunately there was fairly good cover against rifle fire, and, as I have said before, the Dutch never could hit anything at which they aimed their artillery. A lot of lead was wasted and no harm was done, but we are very much afraid our men will not be able to hold out tomorrow if the Boers get reinforcements and try to cut them off. We cannot spare any men. We have too few already, so they may have to retire, and that is always a dangerous business.

It is rumoured today that General French is coming on through Jacobsdal to our relief, and is burning every Dutch *laager* and homestead that he comes across on the way. Certainly I saw three or four columns of smoke over in the Jacobsdal direction this afternoon, but I guess the rumour was made to fit them, for, as far as we know, French is over Colesberg way still. A rumour that Cronje has been captured is probably equally false. It is too good to be true.

Early this morning Major Rodger, the second in command of our mounted men, got shot by the Boers when out with a scouting party in the Alexandersfontein direction. He is a very good man, a keen sportsman, a first-rate shot, and full of the quiet, determined pluck that the men appreciate far better than hot-headed recklessness. They would follow him anywhere. He had sent some men to spy out the land behind some *kopjes*, and after a time saw two men coming out on the far side. Thinking they were his own men, he rode off towards them, well in advance of the main body. When he got within about seventy yards, he saw that they were Boers. If he returned to his own men, he knew the Boers would shoot, *ditto* if he galloped up to them, and if he tried to get his revolver out of the holster, they would certainly pot him before he could fire; so he pulled his horse into a walk and went right up to them. When quite close, one of them spoke to him in Dutch:

"Who are you?"

"Oh, I am one of the fighting men from Kimberley," he answered.

The words were hardly out of his mouth before the gallant pair of Boers turned round and fled over the *veldt* for all they were worth. When they got about half a mile away, they came up to some of their own men hidden in a *sluit*, and then they all fired at Rodger together, but in the meantime his men had come up, and after a volley or two the Boers suddenly remembered that it was breakfast-time and went off. Rodger was hit in the left forearm and one of the bones broken, but he went on and finished his day's work, and only came to look for me at half-past five in the afternoon. I was out, so Mackenzie saw him and wanted to order him off duty, but Rodger flatly declined, and I don't expect he will appear on the sick list at all. The Regulars call our Kimberley forces "tin soldiers," and are a little inclined to be superior with them, but if this is a sample, the tin breed is the one for us.

I was down the Kimberley Mine when Rodger was looking for me. I had an hour or so to spare, and thought I would see if I could be of any help down there, though Mackenzie had been down in the morning. Still, I knew that there were a lot of small ailments amongst the people there, and, as they had been down for three days, a second visit would not hurt them.

I got to the mine just as they were sending the tea down. There were a thousand people to be fed, but the Company was quite equal to it. A staff of their ambulance men had been put on duty, and they were sending down huge quantities of corned-beef sandwiches (in condensed milk boxes for convenience in handling), and buckets of tea and coffee, with condensed milk in it. This was at a time when nobody above ground could get either corned (tinned) beef or condensed milk without a doctor's order, and as there was a fair supply of fresh milk for the children, those down below fared better than those above. I went first down to the lowest level, fifteen hundred feet below the surface. As well as I know the mine, I was astonished to see how different it looked full of people. They were in the large chamber cut in the rock, past one end of which the shaft runs. It is about twenty feet high and thirty or forty wide, and leads away into the mine at the far end.

It was lighted up as usual with electric light, and was fairly cool, but it was just packed with people. Most of the children had been laid down to sleep on the rugs and blankets or mattresses they had brought with them, and these things just covered the floor. Except for a passage down the whole length of the chamber, there did not seem to be an inch of space. I moved about gingerly for fear of treading on somebody, and saw a few people who had little troubles or wanted to know how things were up above, but the people were as good as gold and did not make a single complaint. Many of the babies were a little feverish from the draughts, which were unavoidable, and from the rather close atmosphere, but this was far better than I had expected, considering the number of people.

Except those who were looking after things, I hardly saw a man there. A few had come down at first, but public opinion had got rid of them by this time. I spent some time here talking to the people I knew. Many of them asked whether I advised them to stay down or not. I said that if they were well, I thought they should stay, but if they were feeling seedy and had a decently strong shelter up above, I advised them to go up, as there were often long intervals between the shells, during which they could get food, fresh air, a bath, and so on.

Then I went up to the next level, twelve hundred feet down, and found things just about the same, only it was cooler and the people were, if anything, packed closer. Walking round and dodging the sleeping babies reminded me of a visit I made to that place near Brigg where the seagulls nest. There you could hardly put a foot down without damaging eggs or young birds, and it was just the same here.

After looking round, I went up top-side again, and found more people there in the tunnel, which slopes down from the compound to the cage in which the boys go down the mine. The bottom end of this is about thirty feet below the ground, but opens into a large space round the engine-house, so that many people who did not care to go down below took shelter here, as they could get out into the air between the spells of shelling. But this place had many drawbacks. It was only about three feet wide, and when you lay down, people kept walking over you all the time, so it was not really so good as the mine.

I forgot to tell you, when speaking of the provisions captured at Alexandersfontein, that many of our men carried off anything that came handy in the eatable line. Some of them were busy chivvying fowls and turkeys even when the Boer fire was hottest. But the butter was the greatest attraction. Most of it was commandeered by the military for the hospital, but I know of one man getting away with two pounds by sticking it on his arm and wrapping a handkerchief round it, and putting the whole thing into a sling as if he were wounded. Others came in with fowls and ducks slung across their saddles in regular campaigning style.

CHAPTER 11

Relief at Last

Today (February 15th) is almost too good to write about. Yesterday we were very sceptical about French's advance, and to-night he is here, having brought his men along one hundred and twenty miles in four days. It is almost too good to believe, and no one can realise what it means yet, it has been so unexpected. But I had better finish the story of the siege properly, having got so far. Last night at about ten o'clock we heard heavy rifle firing out at Carter's Farm and Otto's Kopje, and a Maxim got to work too. The Maxim is easy to identify at a distance. It sounds like a street boy running along your freshly painted garden railings with a stick. We wondered what on earth was happening. Had the Boers at last plucked up courage to attack?

The rattle only lasted about half an hour, so evidently there was nothing very serious. In the morning we found that it had just been a little ruse to divert the Boers' minds, and keep their attention fixed whilst our men brought in the captured provisions from Alexandersfontein. We wanted them too badly to risk losing them for want of a little strategy, and that which we practised was quite successful. I got my share of yesterday's loot in the shape of three very large onions and a couple of vegetable marrows, and they were just lovely.

The big gun started at about ten o'clock, and the cordite gun at Carter's put in a good deal of work too. This latter scared me badly during the morning, as I had to see a lot of patients in the district to which it was paying particular attention. I somehow felt that relief was close at hand, as the rumours of French's advance were very persistent this morning, and yet, though no shell came near me, I could not get over a horrid feeling that it would be just my luck to get bowled over at the last moment, after going scot-free for so long.

At one house where I called I could not make any one hear at the front door, so I went round to the back-yard gate, where I found all the children busy digging out a shell which had dropped there a few minutes before, but the patient was safe in the house fort. This was the last shell that small gun fired, and I think the big gun only put one more in before it retired from business altogether. All the morning we kept hearing that the Boers were trying all they knew to rout our men out of Alexandersfontein, but they did not seem altogether big enough for the job, and we hoped to let it stay at that, but were anxious all the same.

At about half-past three o'clock in the afternoon a man told me that French's column could be seen from the Beaconsfield *débris* heaps, but I did not believe it until I went over to the club and found that it was quite true. Then I went straight away and bought the largest Union Jack I could get hold of, and Agnes tied it on a long stick and stuck it out from the end of our second-story verandah for all the world to admire. We ourselves admired it more than anything else on the face of the earth just then.

After that I drove up on to the *veldt* about a mile, out to a place where one could get a view of the surrounding country, and had a good look round. In several directions there were clouds of dust, showing that big bodies of men were on the move, but though the relief-work natives there declared they were English, it was impossible to be sure.

(Somehow I have forgotten to mention those relief works. They were started by Mr. Rhodes quite early in the siege. The roads of one part of the town, which had only been acquired by the De Beers Company a few months ago, were shockingly bad, so when it became necessary to find something for natives, and others who had "got no work to do," to make a living wage at, they were turned on to these roads, and several thousands of them have been working ever since, and besides making a living for themselves, have wonderfully improved that part of the town.)

Finding that nothing could be seen from where I was, I came home to fetch Agnes, and started for Beaconsfield, in which direction it seemed most probable that our troops would arrive, but when I was passing the hospital gate I saw the ambulance go in. As my post was there when there were any wounded around, I went to see what was happening, and found two fresh wounded cases. I told Agnes where to get the best view in Beaconsfield, and sent her off alone. Both the wounded were shot in the head. One had a depressed fracture of the

129

skull, and I had to trephine and remove some splinters of bone that were driven in, but it was quite a simple, straightforward case, and the man will probably recover without a hitch of any sort.

The other was a most interesting case. The patient, a boy of twelve, had been playing about on the outskirts of the Alexandersfontein fighting, picking up bits of shell and other unconsidered trifles, and generally having a good time. But at last I suppose he got too venture-some and went to pick up some shell within range of the Boer rifles, and they potted him right through the head, from above the right eye to above and behind the left ear. He was very collapsed, and brain was oozing out of both wounds. If it had been six months ago, I should have said he would certainly die, but I know Mauser bullets better now, and should not be surprised if he pulled through all right.

By the time I had fixed him up, it was nearly dark, and I had missed the actual entry of the relief column, but I was in time to see the ar-rival of General French and his staff in the town. Agnes had seen the whole thing down in Beaconsfield, and had been one of the group of ladies who nearly pulled the first man in off his horse, they were so delighted to see him. The scene in the town and at the club can't be described. I am not going to try to do it, but it was quieter than you would have expected; everybody was far too deeply moved to be noisy.

Directly the relief was an established fact, they began to haul up the people from the mines, and they were all up by about midnight, none the worse for their four days' stay down below.

And so our siege is over, and though we have had nothing like so bad a time as Mafeking and Ladysmith, if all we hear about them is true, still it was quite bad enough. We all feel just what a friend said to me tonight:

If ever I am in a country where they begin to talk about war again, I shall take the first boat to the far side of the world, and stop when I get there.

We have been shut up for one hundred and twenty-four days (from October 14th to February 15th), and during the whole of this time the Boers have never once attacked the town, or even been within rifle shot of it. Through their friends in town, they must have known almost to a man the strength of our defence forces, and yet they have contented themselves with shelling us from a distance.

It is funny to see in the Dutch papers how every general is alluded to as "Fighting" General Snyman or De la Rey, or whatever his name may be. We wonder whether there are other classes of generals— "praying" generals, or perhaps even "funking" generals.

I spoke of our defence forces just now; it will interest you to know who and what they were:—Mounted men: Kimberley Light Horse, 335; Cape Police, about 300; Diamond Fields Horse, about 150. This makes a total of 785, but what with sickness, guards on barriers, cattle guards, etc., we could never turn out more than 550 for any offensive measures against the Boers, and as they were all mounted, infantry was not of much use against them. Next came the artillery:—Diamond Fields Artillery, 118; Royal Artillery, 95—213 in all; then the infantry:—Town Guard, 2794; Lancashires, roughly, 500; Kimberley Rifles, 380—a total of 3674.

Out of the total number of available defenders (4,672), only about 600 were Regulars, or 900 including the police, and therefore we feel proud of ourselves, as our own men have done so much towards the defence of our own town. But the two men of whom we are most proud are Colonel Kekewich and Mr, Rhodes—of the colonel for the even-handed justice with which he has administered everything for the benefit of rich and poor alike, and of Mr. Rhodes for the magnificent way in which he has acted as a guardian angel to us all.

LEONAUR

ALSO FROM LEONAUR
AVAILABLE IN SOFTCOVER OR HARDCOVER WITH DUST JACKET

THE 9TH—THE KING'S (LIVERPOOL REGIMENT) IN THE GREAT WAR 1914 - 1918 *by Enos H. G. Roberts*—Mersey to mud—war and Liverpool men.

THE GAMBARDIER *by Mark Severn*—The experiences of a battery of Heavy artillery on the Western Front during the First World War.

FROM MESSINES TO THIRD YPRES *by Thomas Floyd*—A personal account of the First World War on the Western front by a 2/5th Lancashire Fusilier.

THE IRISH GUARDS IN THE GREAT WAR - VOLUME 1 *by Rudyard Kipling*—Edited and Compiled from Their Diaries and Papers—The First Battalion.

THE IRISH GUARDS IN THE GREAT WAR - VOLUME 1 *by Rudyard Kipling*—Edited and Compiled from Their Diaries and Papers—The Second Battalion.

ARMOURED CARS IN EDEN *by K. Roosevelt*—An American President's son serving in Rolls Royce armoured cars with the British in Mesopatamia & with the American Artillery in France during the First World War.

CHASSEUR OF 1914 *by Marcel Dupont*—Experiences of the twilight of the French Light Cavalry by a young officer during the early battles of the great war in Europe.

TROOP HORSE & TRENCH *by R.A. Lloyd*—The experiences of a British Lifeguardsman of the household cavalry fighting on the western front during the First World War 1914-18.

THE EAST AFRICAN MOUNTED RIFLES *by C.J. Wilson*—Experiences of the campaign in the East African bush during the First World War.

THE LONG PATROL *by George Berrie*—A Novel of Light Horsemen from Gallipoli to the Palestine campaign of the First World War.

THE FIGHTING CAMELIERS *by Frank Reid*—The exploits of the Imperial Camel Corps in the desert and Palestine campaigns of the First World War.

STEEL CHARIOTS IN THE DESERT *by S. C. Rolls*—The first world war experiences of a Rolls Royce armoured car driver with the Duke of Westminster in Libya and in Arabia with T.E. Lawrence.

WITH THE IMPERIAL CAMEL CORPS IN THE GREAT WAR *by Geoffrey Inchbald*—The story of a serving officer with the British 2nd battalion against the Senussi and during the Palestine campaign.